COMPILED BY DAVID CLIFFORD

First Published 1997

ISBN 1 900467 02 X

Produced by
Finial Publishing
36 Park Road
Swanage BH19 2AD
England
Tel/Fax: 01929 423980

in collaboration with
The Flying Scotsman Association
The Medawar Centre
Oxford Science Park
Oxford OX4 4GA
England
Tel: 01865 784600
e-mail: vbuddin@oxmol.co.uk

Reprographics
Dorset Scanning Services Ltd
Poole, Dorset BH17 7BX
England

Printed by
Wincanton Print Company Ltd
Wincanton, Somerset BA9 9RR
England

Distributed in Australia &
New Zealand by
Railmac Publications
PO Box 290, Elizabeth,
South Australia 5112
Tel: (08) 8255 9446
Fax: (08) 8287 0696
RMPN 116

Photograph: No.4472 pictured at Eastleigh MPD on 18 May 1963 shortly after preservation.

THE WORLD'S MOST
STEAM LOCOM

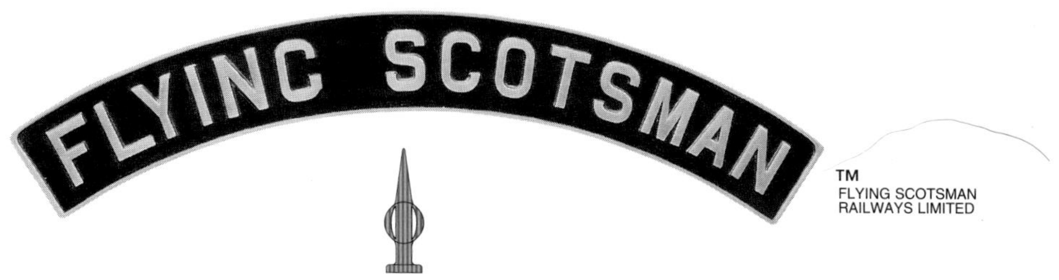

FINIAL PUBLISHING

IN COLLABORATION WITH THE FLYING SCOTSMAN ASSOCIATION

Alan Pegler

In December 1962, the forthcoming withdrawal of *Flying Scotsman* was duly announced and I bought her. She was the first main line express locomotive ever to be privately purchased with the intention of being kept running, a concept that was considered quite revolutionary at the time. She made her last BR service run on 14 January 1963, working the 13.15 King's Cross-Leeds service as far as Doncaster. I then had her put through the Works from which she had first emerged almost exactly 40 years earlier and had the single chimney restored, together with the LNER green livery and the number she had carried for nearly 22 years - 4472.

She ran various trials in March 1963 and made her first run as a privately owned locomotive, hauling a chartered BR passenger train on Saturday 20 April 1963 from Paddington to Ruabon in North Wales for the Festiniog Railway Society. She worked the return train to Paddington from Shrewsbury in the small hours of Sunday 21 April.

Her most celebrated 'specials' were the non-stop runs from King's Cross-Edinburgh and back in May 1968, 40 years to the day after the non-stop run she had inaugurated in 1928. Both runs were completed without stopping, but this could only be accomplished by having a second tender carrying an additional 6,000 gallons of water.

During the 10 years I owned the locomotive, the background to the nameplates was painted red. This was on the initiative of the foreman of the paint shop at Doncaster who had been told by Gresley he was going to have special red nameplates for special locomotives such as *Silver Link* and *Mallard*, but which never actually happened due to the outbreak of war in 1939. The traditional black background was reverted to in 1973.

She went to North America from the Autumn of 1969 until February 1973, Mr 'Bill' (now the Hon Sir William) McAlpine bringing her back from California after my money had run out. Sir William owned and ran *Flying Scotsman* for 23 years during which time the locomotive was involved in working many further main line special trains in Great Britain. She also made a spectacular visit to Australia during which she set yet another record, a non-stop run of no less than 422 miles, one which will surely never now be broken. That trip to Down Under was completed just before Christmas 1989.

In early 1996, it was decided to put *Flying Scotsman* up for sale. The locomotive was bought by Dr A F (Tony) Marchington in February of that year, almost 73 years to the day since she had first entered regular service with the LNER in 1923.

Dr Marchington immediately put in hand the full repair programme which had been put on hold in 1995, with a view to having the work completed in 1998 - *Flying Scotsman's* 75th birthday year. His hope is to keep the locomotive running well into the 21st Century, something that had been my long term aim back in 1963.

Alan Pegler

The Hon Sir William McAlpine Bt

The romantic age when steam was an everyday occurrence, has gone forever, only the preserved railways in Britain and around the world - and a few legendary steam locomotives - remaining as reminders. However, the name *Flying Scotsman* will always be first whenever the vintage days of railway travel are recalled.

Flying Scotsman is not only the world's most famous steam locomotive, it is also the world's most travelled locomotive, having visited not only just about every major city and town in Britain, but also during 1969-1973, the huge cities, mountains and prairies of the United States of America and Canada.

Additionally, following an invitation from the Aus Steam '88 Committee, I agreed for the locomotive to be a guest at the celebration of Australia's Bi-Centennial Year in 1988. The Committee had undertaken the management of the visit and also produced an itinerary allowing the locomotive to visit all mainland states. As history records, the visit to Australia was an outstanding success, the locomotive setting several new world records during its travels around the continent.

Because of the visit to Australia, *Flying Scotsman* enhanced its reputation even further as the world's most famous steam locomotive and in the process, secured for itself the accolade of becoming, without a shadow of doubt, the world's most travelled steam locomotive.

Everyone with an eye for railway beauty and poetry of motion, has admired *Flying Scotsman*, the superb creation of Sir Nigel Gresley. Almost from the time the locomotive was first constructed, the LNER cared for No.4472 with reverence and pride and before the paint was hardly dry, the locomotive attracted the attention of the public. Largely as a result of No.4472 *Flying Scotsman's* association with the parent company's train of the same name, No.4472 became a symbol of power and prestige during the lifetime of the LNER. Unfortunately, after the nationalisation of British Railways in 1948, these loyalties were gradually dissipated and with the demise of steam traction on BR, the eventual fate of the vast majority of Britain's steam locomotives became only too apparent.

Surprisingly, it was left to the embryonic railway preservation movement to ensure that *Flying Scotsman* survived, at the time economics rather than sentiment dictating official preservation policy. Fortunately, Alan Pegler saved *Flying Scotsman* for the nation - indeed the world - and early in 1973 I was privileged to take over that responsibility. That responsibility has now been handed to Dr Tony Marchington and who knows what further exciting adventures await *Flying Scotsman* in the years to come.

On 10 January 1921, Great Northern Railway Engine Order No.293 was issued giving Doncaster Works authority to construct two Pacific locomotives. Apart from the construction of 4-6-2 tank locomotives, this was only the second time that a 4-6-2 wheel arrangement had been used in Great Britain for an express passenger locomotive - the first had been the Great Western Railway's *Great Bear* No.111 completed at Swindon in February 1908. The frames for the new Pacific were laid down in the new Erecting Shop at Doncaster for the first of these - No.1470 - on 26 August 1921 and for No.1471 four days later.

No.1470 was mechanically completed on 25 March 1922 and ex-works on 30 March. Appropriately named *Great Northern*, No.1470 entered traffic on 11 April 1922. Evidence of early satisfaction with the 4-6-2 design, came with an order for a further 10 Pacifics on 10 July 1922, the day No.1471 - later named *Sir Frederick Banbury* - entered traffic.

On 7 February 1923, No.1472 (Works No.1564) - the first of the batch of 10 4-6-2 Pacifics authorised on 10 July the previous year - made its debut from Doncaster Works. Equipped with 180lb per square inch boiler No.7693 - ordered in August 1922 - the locomotive was married to eight-wheeled tender No.5223, the completed locomotive costing £7,944 to construct.

Although essentially of GNR origin and virtually completed before the official inauguration of the LNER, No.1472's place in history was assured from the start. Not only was it the first passenger locomotive to be outshopped from Doncaster Works under the auspices of the LNER, it was the first locomotive to proudly wear the new standard Apple-Green livery.

Consequently, it was no surprise, that the as-yet unnamed No.1472, found itself paraded at Marylebone on 22 February 1923, at the start of a career which would take it around the globe and earn it the title 'the world's most famous steam locomotive'.

SIR NIGEL GRESLEY
Chief Mechanical Engineer
London & North Eastern Railway 1923 - 1941
Geoffrey Hughes' Collection

LEFT: The first of Gresley's new Pacifics emerged from Doncaster at the beginning of April 1922, appropriately named *Great Northern*. With the temporary suffix 'N' added, No.1470 is pictured leaving King's Cross.
P N Townend Collection.

RIGHT: The spacious cab of the Pacific bears testimony to the affinity Sir Nigel Gresley had with the men that drove and fired his locomotives, the traditional GNR footplate providing some of the most spartan conditions on any British railway up to that time. The commodious side-windowed cab was a completely new concept on the GNR and the controls were so arranged that the driver could drive the engine from a seated position. The 'padded' seats later gave way to 'bucket' seats, which were even more of an improvement.
P N Townend Collection.

Constructional work on a vast site at Wembley north-east of London had been inaugurated in 1922 for the British Empire Exhibition, one of the most ambitious displays ever conceived. The Great Exhibition itself would not be officially opened until over two years later and with the 1923 Grouping of the British railway network intervening, it is unclear just how much importance the four new main line railway companies placed on the event. However, what was evident was the fact that the Grouping had least affected the Great Western Railway and it was also realised that Sir Felix Pole - the General Manager of the GWR at that period - would not pass up the opportunity to publicise his Company and equipment.

No.4073 *Caerphilly Castle*, the first of the GWR's much-vaunted four-cylinder 4-6-0 Castle class locomotives had made its debut at Paddington station on 23 August 1923. No.4073 had been the first locomotive outshopped from Swindon Works since the Great War with the lined-out panels and boiler-bands, polished brass cab number plates and splasher beadings which had always previously characterised GW locomotives and the LNER realised that they had been set a hard act to follow. The advent of nine more Castles from Swindon Works, marked a further shift towards pre-war standards of painting and adornment, the full lining-out which had been abandoned as a war-time expedient being restored, together with polished brass safety valve bonnets and polished copper tops to the chimneys.

Gresley knew only too well what the GWR were capable of and the magnificent publicity which would be offered by the British Empire Exhibition. He determined not to be outdone and on 27 December 1923, No.1472 entered Doncaster Works for general repair, being outshopped on 2 March 1924, externally a very different locomotive! First of all, following on from an instruction dated 6 February 1924, to add 3000 to all existing GNR numbers, No.1472's running number had been changed to 4472. Equally significant, the previously unnamed locomotive now proudly bore the nameplates *Flying Scotsman*, clearly a reference to the long-standing London King's Cross-Edinburgh Waverley express of the same name, a name which had been in popular use from about 1862.

The pride of Doncaster Works, No.4472 was especially painted and embellished for display at the Exhibition. An LNER crest had been placed on each cabside, brass trim attached to the splashers and the locomotive's tyres brightly burnished. Because of this special finish, a full-length protective hessian cover was manufactured to almost completely cover the engine and tender during the transfer of the locomotive south from Doncaster to London.

For display at the first Exhibition in 1924, No.4472 was coupled to its own GNR-type eight-wheeled tender with 'LNER' surmounting the number '4472' on the tender sides.

So it was, on the 23 April 1924, the much vaunted British Empire Exhibition was opened by King George V, which apart from a break during the winter months, continued until October 1925, in the process attracting some 26,000,000 visitors. During the first year of the Exhibition, the GWR proudly displayed the first of the Castle class of locomotives No.4073 *Caerphilly Castle*. The LNER exhibited Gresley Pacific No.4472 *Flying Scotsman* and by way of contrast, No.1 *Locomotion* of the Stockton & Darlington Railway.

For many visitors to the Exhibition, the sight of the LNER and GWR flagship locomotives on display back-to-back with each other must have been impressive. To the casual observer, there can have been little doubt about the capabilities of each locomotive. With extra wheels, higher boiler and vast firebox, the Gresley Pacific almost dwarfed the Castle, a comparison further accentuated by the eight-wheeled tender of No.4472. What then of the notice displayed before the GWR Castle proclaiming it to be 'the most powerful passenger engine in Britain', a claim based on tractive effort, the Castle boasting 31,625lb, compared to the Gresley Pacific's 29,835lb. These visual impressions contradicting the bravura powers claimed by the GWR for *Caerphilly Castle* and its stable-mates, a contest of some sort appeared inevitable and in the Spring of 1925, the famous LNER versus GWR interchanges took place, both Companies hoping to prove the superiority of their locomotive.

TOP: Without nameplates, No.4472 is pictured heading north from York. *P N Townend Collection.*

RIGHT: A gleaming testimonial to the LNER, No.4472 in pristine condition, with highly burnished tyres and motion and with brightly polished copper and brass fittings, awaits public acclaim before the opening of the first British Empire Exhibition in 1924. *Gresley Society Collection.*

FLYING SCOTSMAN
4472

ABOVE: Acutely aware of the importance and benefits of good publicity, the LNER was careful to promote its strengths with special newsworthy events for the benefit of the press and through newsreels. One such event took place in 1927 - the year the Romney Hythe & Dymchurch Railway opened. As part of a publicity campaign to promote the RH&DR (and the LNER), one-third size 15in.-gauge RH&DR locomotive Pacific No.7 *Typhoon*, was taken to 'Top Shed' King's Cross to pose alongside Gresley Pacific No.4472 *Flying Scotsman*, still in Exhibition condition. *P N Townend Collection*.

ABOVE: Tender piled high with coal and still resplendent in full Exhibition livery, No.4472 is prepared for its next turn of duty on the turntable at Doncaster Works. The five Work's employees - including the youngster on the footplate (probably an apprentice) - are all clearly enjoying having their photograph taken for posterity with the most prestigious of their Company's fleet of locomotives. ***John P Robinson Collection.***

1925 would prove a significant milestone in the annals of British railway history, several important events taking place. Early in the year, No.4472 *Flying Scotsman* could be found going about its duties on the GN main line, polished brightwork and coat-of-arms on cab sides - striking reminders of the locomotive's appearance at the British Empire Exhibition the previous year - making identification a simple matter.

Firstly, following a 'friendly' interchange of locomotives between the LNER and the GWR for a week - starting 27 April - Gresley Pacific No.4474 (at that time unnamed) worked over GW metals and No.4475 (recently named *Flying Fox*) stayed on home territory. The GW despatched No.4079 *Pendennis Castle* to the LNER, while No.4074 *Caldicot Castle* stayed on home ground. The performances by No.4079 *Pendennis Castle* between King's Cross and Grantham/Doncaster on alternative test days, forced the reluctant acceptance by the LNER that the GWR had acquitted themselves well, with the Pacific's original valve gear settings proving inferior to that fitted to the GWR Castles.

The second important event of 1925 would be the re-opening of the British Empire Exhibition at Wembley. The LNER chose the same locomotive - No.4472 *Flying Scotsman* - but almost as if to rub salt into the wounds of the LNER, the GWR chose to exhibit No.4079 *Pendennis Castle*. All the exhibits would remain on display at Wembley until 31 October 1925, when the Exhibition finally closed.

ABOVE: No.4472 being prepared for the re-opening of the British Empire Exhibition in May 1925. As resplendent as ever, *Flying Scotsman* on this occasion had been coupled temporarily to smaller K3 6-wheel tender No.5358, apparently due to the more limited exhibition space which was available. *Gresley Society Collection.*

RIGHT: The fine lines of Gresley's Pacific class of locomotive is shown to its full effect in this classic photograph taken in 1936. Outside King's Cross 'Top Shed', *Flying Scotsman* awaits the next turn of duty, a wisp of steam just visible from both safety valves, tender piled high with coal. Meanwhile, a fitter's assistant makes his way gingerly along the running plate of the locomotive, one hand on the hand rail, the other firmly holding onto a large can of oil, ready to fill the locomotive's lubricators.
Kelland Collection, Bournemouth Railway Club

N E R
4472
472

Because of the adverse performance of the Gresley 4-6-2s in the 1925 locomotive exchanges with the GWR, modifications were made to bring about the better use of steam by the valve gear and cylinders and improve performance by the fitting of long-travel valves. At the same time as these modifications were carried out on No.4472 - February-April 1928 - the locomotive was converted to the standard LNER loading gauge and fitted with a corridor tender in readiness for the inaugural non-stop service between King's Cross and Edinburgh which took place on 1 May 1928.

The day dawned to find huge crowds already assembled at King's Cross to watch the departure from Platform 10 of the Down inaugural non-stop. Similar scenes were taking place at Edinburgh Waverley as No.2580 *Shotover* prepared to depart simultaneously on its non-stop journey south. Promptly at 10.00, a pristine No.4472 - with 'Top Shed' Driver Albert Pibworth - on the footplate, began the long haul northwards. All along the line crowds watched intently as *Flying Scotsman* fleetly went on its way north, while at Tollerton - the change-over point - Gateshead Driver Tom Blades and his firemen made their way through the narrow corridor in the tender to play their part in this historic event.

At 18.03, *Flying Scotsman* arrived at Edinburgh Waverley, a distance of 392.7 miles in 8 hours 3 minutes - a fairly leisurely speed of 47.7 mph - but still with an estimated two tons of coal left in the tender. The following day, 2 May, No.4472 worked the Up 'Flying Scotsman' from Edinburgh to King's Cross.

LEFT: A general view of *Flying Scotsman* showing the corridor exit at the back of the tender.
P N Townend Collection.

RIGHT: Preparing to meet the public, No.4472 *Flying Scotsman* receives last minute checks before joining its train ready for the inaugural non-stop 'Flying Scotsman' on 1 May 1928.
P N Townend Collection.

L N E R
4472
207

Following the fitting of long travel valves and the re-designing of other components, improvements in economy were impressive, narrow piston valve rings instead of the previous broad rings which had been fitted, proving much more steam tight. The modifications helped to reduce coal consumption by enabling the driver to run at shorter cut-offs and there was less steam wastage due to the narrow piston valve rings.

LEFT: Circa 1928 with the train of the same name, *Flying Scotsman* in full flight on the gradient out of King's Cross near Copenhagen Tunnel.

ABOVE: On the exit from King's Cross, No.4472's exhaust stains the sky as it heads north near Gas Works Tunnel. *P N Townend Collection*.

In April 1929, *Flying Scotsman* was in for another taste of stardom, being used throughout during the making of the British International Pictures film 'Flying Scotsman', which would appear in British cinemas the following year. *Flying Scotsman* co-starred with Moore Marriott (who acted the part of the driver), Ray Milland (fireman) and Pauline Johnson (the heroine).

The A1 was in its original condition, with right hand drive and there were only a few studio mock-ups of the footplate for dialogue purposes, these being added later. The film was originally a silent picture, but the 'talkies' arrived during its production and the sound was added to the last two reels to put it out as part talking. This was the first ever sound feature film and included some wonderful shots of *Flying Scotsman*.

The film also upset Gresley, because the runaway train portrayed in the film appeared to lack vacuum brakes and Gresley insisted that a title be put on at the start of the film to say that: 'dramatic licence has been taken for film purposes and does not represent the actual safety equipment used by the LNER'.

Continuing to consolidate its position as 'the world's most famous steam locomotive', on 30 November 1934, No.4472 was set another task, ie to prove that steam power could match the startling advances being made in railway speed at that time, in Germany by diesel-electric power and in the USA with diesel haulage.

Thus it was on a dull November morning, that *Flying Scotsman* found itself at the head of a short four-coach train at King's Cross. On the footplate was Driver Bill Sparshatt and Fireman Webster, their brief being to prove that estimates given by a German manufacturer for the reliable operation of a three-car diesel-electric train between London and Newcastle could be matched by steam. To test his theory, Gresley had instigated two experiments with Pacifics, an A1 being turned out for the run between King's Cross-Leeds and return and an A3 for the full King's Cross-Newcastle run.

On the Down journey with the A1 (*Flying Scotsman*) between King's Cross-Leeds, Driver Sparshatt had not allowed his locomotive to exceed 95 mph, even so, Leeds was reached in 2 hours 31 minutes 56 seconds. However, it was on the Up journey that *Flying Scotsman* secured another place for itself in the annals of railway history, for a close inspection of the dynamometer car roll revealed that for a short distance, No.4472 had reached 100mph, the first authenticated 100mph by a steam locomotive.

ABOVE: *Flying Scotsman* pictured in early BR livery and numbered E103 on an express train duty at Finsbury Park in March 1948.
Rail Archive Stephenson/Photomatic.

Altogether, a total of 79 of the 4-6-2 Pacific class of locomotives similar to *Flying Scotsman* were constructed by the LNER between April 1922 and January 1935, the last batches - consisting of 27 locomotives - built as new with higher pressure 220lb psi boilers as Class A3.

Although the first conversion of an A1 to A3 (No.4480) had taken place in 1927, it would not be until the start of the Second World War, that a start would be made on rebuilding the remainder with 220lb psi boilers and eventually all except one of the original 52 A1s would be converted, *Flying Scotsman* being outshopped with a 220lb psi boiler in January 1947.

The Second World War saw sterling service by *Flying Scotsman* and the rest of the Gresley Pacifics. The war was no respecter of locomotive pedigrees, the Pacifics being pressed into use on goods duties as well as passenger and troop services.

In April 1945, *Flying Scotsman* and all the remaining A1s still carrying 180lb psi boilers were reclassified as A10, the A1 classification being required for a new class of locomotive designed by Edward Thompson who had succeeded Sir Nigel Gresley as CME of the LNER on Gresley's death in April 1941. The influence of Thompson was evident in other ways and even before the nationalisation of the British railway network, the whole of the LNER fleet of locomotives had been renumbered. On 20 January 1946, *Flying Scotsman's* running number had been changed to 502, to be changed on 5 May the same year to 103.

Soon after the formation of BR, *Flying Scotsman* emerged from Doncaster Works on 15 March 1948 bearing the running number E103 (the 'E' denoting the Eastern Region) and with the tender now emblazoned with BRITISH RAILWAYS in large capitals on both sides.

Later in 1948, BR announced that as locomotives passed through the workshops, their numbers would be changed, so that a standard nation-wide numeration would exist regardless of 'regions' and former owners, with all LNER locomotives having 60,000 added to their existing numbers. Consequently, when *Flying Scotsman* emerged from Doncaster Works on 30 December 1948, it bore the running number 60103, the number carried for the rest of its life under public ownership.

Similarly, this was a period when liveries were subject to change. In April 1943, *Flying Scotsman* had been painted in standard wartime black livery and it would be not be until January 1947 that the locomotive would once again wear with pride LNER Apple-Green livery. Even this would be short-lived and following a decision by BR to paint the most powerful express passenger locomotives in a controversial new livery, No.60103 was outshopped in blue with black-and-white lining, a livery carried between overhauls at Doncaster Works between December 1949 and March 1952, No.60103 then receiving BR Green livery, which it carried until withdrawal in January 1963.

ABOVE: No.60103 in BR livery pictured at York shed on 5 September 1954. *Frank Hornby.*

Although No.2751 *Humorist* had been fitted with a 'Kylchap' twin-orifice blastpipe and chimney in 1937, no attempt had been made to modify the remainder of the A1 (later A10) or A3 locomotives in the same way. However, four of the Gresley class A4 locomotives - including No.4468 *Mallard* - had been thus fitted from new, the rest of the A4s being converted during May 1957-November 1958. Following on from the success of these conversions, instructions were given to convert the A3s at an estimated cost of £153 per locomotive.

LEFT: In the 1950s, the Down 'Talisman' is hauled up the gradient from King's Cross by single chimneyed No.60103, while double-chimneyed Gresley A4 No.60023 *Golden Eagle* waits for the road. Clearly illustrated in this photograph of *Flying Scotsman* is the so-called 'Banjo' dome, an improved form of steam collector which was first fitted to No.2500 *Windsor Lad* in 1934 and later fitted to most of the class.
P N Townend.

RIGHT: Circa 1960, on the same train, No.60103 *Flying Scotsman* - by now with double chimney - appears to be making light work of the exit from King's Cross.
P N Townend.

THE TALISMAN
60103
60103

60103
34A
60103

LEFT: Looking the worst for wear, No.60103 is seen receiving attention to its motion in the erecting shops at Doncaster Works on Sunday 20 March 1960. Of interest in this photograph, is the removal of the square pad on the side of the upper part of the smokebox. This was an outward distinguishing mark to indicate that the locomotive was fitted with a high pressure boiler, or more correctly a 43-element superheater, the pads on each side of the smokebox covering holes which had been cut in the smokebox to accommodate the outer ends of the superheater header. *Gavin W Morrison*.

ABOVE: Only a month later, *Flying Scotsman* presents a very different picture as it shares its home shed with two intruders! In connection with a series of special trains run by railway publisher Ian Allan to Doncaster Works in April 1960, various locomotives had been requested including GWR 4-4-0 *City of Truro* and Midland Compound No.1000 (far left), with No.60103 *Flying Scotsman* also required to work from Marylebone to Doncaster and back. Because of the relatively poor condition of No.60103's paintwork compared to the almost museum condition of the other two locomotives, Peter Townend who was Shedmaster at King's Cross MPD between 1956-1961, ordered that *Scotsman* be completely repainted locally, a decision which caused some consternation among BR local management. *P N Townend*.

As 'Kylchap' double blastpipes were installed in the A3s, problems were experienced with steam and smoke drifting down the sides of the boiler and obscuring the forward view of the crews, problems not experienced with the streamlined A4s. To try and overcome the problem, experiments were carried out, small smoke deflectors being fitted to four members of the class. These proved unsuccessful and instead larger and more successful German-style smoke deflectors were tried. Eventually, 55 members of the class were fitted with the trough deflectors, No.60103 leaving Doncaster Works on 16 December 1961 equipped in this way.

In 1959 the first A3 was withdrawn and by 1966 all of the class - with the exception of No.60103 - had been scrapped. When considering the limited numbers of locomotives that could be preserved for historical reasons, it had been decided that Sir Nigel Gresley's regime would be represented by No.4468 *Mallard* - the holder of the world record for steam. However, this did not preclude the possibility of purchases by private ventures, as long as a guarantee could be given that prospective owners had somewhere to keep the machine. Despite the best efforts of the 'Gresley A3 Preservation Society' to raise the £3000 required to purchase primarily *Flying Scotsman*, the attempt was doomed to failure, until Alan Pegler - a businessman and also a part-time member of the Eastern Area Board of the British Transport Commission - stepped in.

ABOVE: In final form with double chimney and German-style trough smoke deflectors, No 60103 is pictured leaving Stoke Tunnel on 21 July 1962.
Gavin W Morrison.
RIGHT: Mutually satisfactory arrangements having been made for the private purchase of No.60103 by Alan Pegler, on 14 January 1963 the locomotive is seen at the head of the 1.15 pm King's Cross-Leeds service. Working as far as Doncaster - its last run in BR service - No.60103 would go straight into Doncaster Plant to be prepared for its new owner.
Norman E Preedy.

60103
A-3
60103

X28
4472
L N E R

After working its last service train for BR on 14 January 1963, *Flying Scotsman* emerged from Doncaster Works on 26 March with single blast pipe and chimney and shorn of deflector plates. The locomotive had also been repainted in Apple-Green livery with red-backed nameplates and running number restored to 4472. In addition, the engine was once again coupled to a corridor tender.

LEFT: The first public appearance of the now privately owned *Flying Scotsman* was on Saturday 20 April 1963, when as part of the Festiniog Railway Society's Centenary of Steam 1863-1963 celebrations, No.4472 worked a special train from Paddington as far as Ruabon. Carrying BR head-code 'X28', No.4472 is seen leaving Paddington at 08.23, the train travelling via High Wycombe, Birmingham Snow Hill, Wolverhampton Low Level and Shrewsbury, arriving at Ruabon at approximately 12.30. Despite heavy rainfall, the occasion attracted numerous enthusiasts to the lineside and at Birmingham Snow Hill thousands of spectators were reported. No.4472 returned light to Shrewsbury in order to take over the return special. *B H Jackson/*The Railway Magazine *Archives.*

ABOVE: The next outing by the now privately owned No.4472 would take place a few weeks later on Saturday 18 May 1963. This was organised by the Gainsborough Model Railway Society in conjunction with Alan Pegler (the Society's President), the special picking up passengers at Lincoln, Gainsborough and Retford for Southampton, the route being via Nottingham Victoria, Leicester, Oxford and Basingstoke. Waiting to return its train to Lincoln after servicing, No.4472 - resplendent in new livery - appears very much at home at Eastleigh MPD, steam still being much in evidence at the time. A few months later, No.4472 would be at Eastleigh again, this time as guest of honour at the Depot's Open day on 21 August. *R C Riley.*

No.4472 *Flying Scotsman* was officially transferred to the ownership of Alan Pegler on 16 April 1963 and was based at Doncaster, a lease being initially acquired on a disused engine weigh-house just off the southern end of No.8 Platform at Doncaster - likened by Alan Pegler to having 'the exclusive use of what amounted to a private garage!'.

Because of earlier cooperation between the Gainsborough Model Railway Society and Alan Pegler in organising and running steam-hauled railtours, the GMRS and George Hinchcliffe (the Secretary of the GMRS) joined with Alan Pegler in 1963 to market and organise No.4472's public tours, George and his wife Frances running the operational organisation 'Flying Scotsman Enterprises' with GMRS volunteers providing essential backup with many other aspects of operating these special trains.

At the time of the purchase, Alan Pegler had negotiated with BR a three year running agreement which ensured that the locomotive would stay active on a wide range of main lines, this agreement later being extended for another five years. Many of the routes used by No.4472 during this period, had never before been penetrated by Gresley Pacifics.

ABOVE: Shortly after being sold to Alan Pegler, No.4472 is coaled by hand underneath the redundant coaling tower at King's Cross. ***P N Townend.***

RIGHT: *Flying Scotsman* continued to be in great demand for operating steam excursions and is pictured here exiting Twerton Tunnel with an all Pullman Ian Allan Railtour between London and Ilfracombe via Bath and Bristol Temple Meads on 19 October 1963, the locomotive being serviced at Exmouth Junction. *A Richardson/*The Railway Magazine *Archives.*

IAN ALLAN
RAIL TOUR
1Z78

1964 would see No.4472 in use in many different locations around the country, including forays north of the border and a first visit to South Wales. On 18 March, No.4472 headed south, its destination Cardiff. Alan Pegler had secured control of the Festiniog Railway Company in 1954, the efforts of a new board of directors and the members of the preservation society ensuring that in 1963 record operating figures were achieved. Acknowledging the part that Alan Pegler had played in the resurrection of the FR, the Welsh Tourist Board on 18 March 1964 presented Mr Pegler - as Chairman of the FRC - with the Board's Certificate of Merit for 'conspicuous services to tourism in Wales'. For the journey from Doncaster, Mr Pegler used his own locomotive to haul the 'Festiniog Railway Special', a three-coach train, with stops at Sheffield, Chesterfield, Derby, Saltley and Gloucester. No.4472 carried a head-board decorated with the crest of the FR and on arrival at Cardiff, Mr Pegler and other directors of the railway were met by the Lord Mayor, who together with officials and guests of the Welsh Tourist Board, went for a short trip in the observation car of the special train. On the return to Cardiff, the presentation was made on the station platform.

Saturday 2 May 1964, saw a flurry of activity with the few Gresley Pacifics which were still extant. A Gresley Society railtour - the 'London North Eastern Flier' - was worked by No.60106 *Flying Fox* between King's Cross and Doncaster in each direction and by No.60103 *Flying Scotsman* from Doncaster-York, York-Darlington and Darlington-Doncaster. The same day No.60051 *Blink Bonny* had worked an RCTS special from the north to York and was recorded as reaching 91mph at one point during the journey.

LEFT: No.4472 arriving at Cardiff on a wintry 18 March 1964. *Allan Garraway.*

RIGHT: No.60051 is pictured alongside No.4472 which was about to depart for Darlington on 2 May 1964. *Gavin W Morrison.*

LONDON
NORTH EASTERN
FLIER
RCTS
60051
L N E R
4472
S11B
S12B

On 9 May 1964, *Flying Scotsman* left Doncaster, heading north in preparation for a foray into Scotland the following weekend. Rather than have No.4472 travel 'light', Alan Pegler hired the complete 'Master Cutler' Pullman set to make the locomotive's return to Scotland a 'really special occasion'.

The train - entitled 'Pegler's Pullman' - left Doncaster at 07.00, enthusiastic crowds greeting *Flying Scotsman* at the various stopping places. Travelling via York, Northallerton, Stockton, Sunderland, Newcastle, Berwick-on-Tweed to Edinburgh Waverley, the train received an official welcome, which was responded to by Alan Pegler. At Waverley, BR Scottish Region sold souvenir platform tickets, all bearing the number 4472, which allowed viewing of the locomotive which was stabled in a Bay platform. The return journey was made behind A4 No.60009 *Union of South Africa*.

During the following week, *Flying Scotsman* took time out to pose for its portrait, the painter - the late Terence Cuneo - executing a painting of the locomotive on the Forth Bridge. The following weekend - Saturday 16 May 1964 - the University of St Andrew's Queen's College Railway & Transport Society had obtained No.4472 to haul a history-making Edinburgh-Aberdeen round trip. This was the locomotive's first visit to Scotland since being privately purchased from BR and was believed to be No.4472's first visit to the 'Granite City'. The route for the outward journey was via Perth and Forfar, returning from Aberdeen via Dundee.

ABOVE: 'Flying Scotsman Crossing the Forth Bridge', by the late Terence Cuneo CVO, OBE, RGI. *Cuneo Fine Arts.*

RIGHT: On 17 August 1964, No.4472 came south hauling a Warwickshire Railway Society special from Sheffield via Chesterfield, Derby and Birmingham to Swindon and Eastleigh for visits to the locomotive works and sheds at both places. *En route* No.4472 continued to attract large crowds. Here, the locomotive climbing Sapperton Bank provides a stirring sight. *Ivo Peters courtesy of Julian Peters.*

WRS
SPECIAL
4472

In November 1964, No.4472 entered Darlington Works for heavy repair and overhaul, every part of the locomotive being stripped down and examined, including the boiler which was replaced. On 23 February 1965, No.4472 emerged from Darlington, working a special test train consisting of a 20 ton brake-van from Darlington to Eaglescliffe, Stockton-on-Tees, West Hartlepool and Sunderland, thence back to Darlington. As work on No.4472 reached completion, the Darlington Locomotive Works Manager - Mr P Gray - in conjunction with Alan Pegler, obtained permission from the British Rail Board to hold an Open Day on Saturday 3 April with *Flying Scotsman* as guest of honour. This proved a highly successful event, all proceeds going to the Derby Railway Orphanage. The following week, on Saturday 10 April 1965, No.4472 made its first official run after overhaul and as a 'thank you' from Alan Pegler, some 120 men who had been engaged in the work at Darlington were taken on a tour of the Fen country using Pullman stock from the 'Tees-Tyne Pullman'.

LEFT: On what would be one of its last excursions before entering Darlington Works for heavy overhaul, No.4472 is pictured at the buffer stops at London King's Cross after hauling a 'Lyons Maid Zoom' special on 30 August 1964. *Brian Stephenson/*The Railway Magazine *Archives*.

RIGHT: A few months after overhaul, *Flying Scotsman* was again to be found at Swindon MPD, this time with the visiting Railway Correspondence & Travel Society 'East Midlander', from Nottingham via Beeston, Leicester and Wellingborough for visits to the Clapham Transport Museum as well as Swindon Works. The scene on Saturday 29 May 1965 clearly illustrates how fast the demise of steam haulage was progressing at this period, the only other steam locomotive in sight being No.4472's protagonist from another period, GWR No.4079 *Pendennis Castle* which was already destined for preservation. *Ivo Peters courtesy of Julian Peters.*

6A22
GREAT WESTERN
4472

LEFT: No. 4472 is seen heading north over the impressive spans of the Lune Viaduct near Sedbergh on the Yorkshire/Westmorland border on Saturday 4 September 1965 as it hauls the Warwickshire Railway Society's 'Pennine Tour' from Birmingham via Derby, Sheffield and Leeds to Carlisle for a visit to Kingmoor MPD. On a typically dull autumn day, in the distance the imposing peak of Arant Haw, standing at 1,989ft above sea level, is shrouded in low cloud and mist.
Ivo Peters courtesy of Julian Peters.

RIGHT: The following weekend - Sunday 12 September 1965 - *Flying Scotsman* hauled a Gainsborough Model Railway Society tour from Waterloo to Weymouth, returning to Paddington via Yeovil. No.4472 is seen being turned on the turntable at Weymouth in preparedness for the return journey.
D E Canning.

Although the owner of No.4472, Alan Pegler was not permitted to drive the locomotive under the agreement he had entered into with BR and at the insistance of the rail unions. Nonetheless, there were still many tasks which would keep him busy.

RIGHT: Amongst piles of slag and ashes outside Weymouth shed, the BR crew responsible for *Flying Scotsman*, give careful attention to oiling the motion of the locomotive before the A3 backs onto its train at Weymouth station in the late afternoon of Sunday 12 September 1965. *D E Canning.*

BELOW: After arriving at Weymouth on Sunday 12 September 1965 with a railtour from Waterloo, Alan Pegler carefully polishes the nameplate of 'the old girl' ready for the return journey to Paddington via Reading. *D E Canning.*

RIGHT: Under darkening skies and with Brunel's distinctive Italianate tower silhouetted in the distance, No.4472 waits at the platforms of Reading station ready to take the GMRS special on the final leg of its journey from Weymouth to Paddington on Sunday 12 September 1965. Despite the obviously late hour, catching some of the aura that surrounds 'the world's most famous steam locomotive', two serious-faced young trainspotters, notebooks and pencils clasped in grubby hands, make their way to the front of the train in anticipation of the departure, while a duffle-coated photographer, camera in hand, his supply of film probably exhausted, turns his back on the scene. *D E Canning.*

THE
GAINSBOROUGH
MODEL RAILWAY
SOCIETY
No. 4472
A3

In the autumn of 1965, *Railway Magazine* announced that on 9 October, it was organising a 'Welsh Mystery Flyer' steam special. Advertised as 'one of the GREAT DAYS for railway enthusiasts', the day included a *Flying Scotsman* hauled run between Paddington and Cardiff in 140 minutes, which included a five minute water stop at Swindon; a six hour 'grand mystery tour' of the Welsh Valleys and from Cardiff a 'record-nudging fast run home' in 120 minutes at 73 mph average speed using a Brush Type 4 Diesel.

With some 300 passengers on the seven-coach train, the 'Welsh Mystery Flyer' hauled by No.4472, left Paddington without any problems becoming apparent. However, on reaching the western fringes of the Vale of White Horse, speed fell off with No.4472 being forced to limp to Swindon, commendably arriving only five minutes behind schedule. On inspection, it was found that the left-hand back steam-chest cover had come completely adrift! The locomotive was immediately failed, being replaced by a Hymek diesel-hydraulic locomotive at very short notice (a note had been thrown out at Uffington signalbox to warn officials of the problems being experienced!). With the Hymek in charge of the train, Cardiff was reached only 15 minutes late.

After the event, Alan Pegler summed-up the situation by stating that 'if a railway engine could blush, the *Flying Scotsman* would have done just that ...' and immediately announced for the benefit of disappointed lineside spectators, that No.4472 would haul a private train - the 'Panda Pullman' (arranged in collaboration with the World Wildlife Fund) - on Saturday 13 November to the 140 minute timing. True to his word, the famous locomotive covered the same route on the date specified and arrived in Cardiff three minutes ahead of schedule, in the process achieving a steam record for the London-Cardiff run which still holds today.

LEFT: The ill-fated 'Welsh Mystery Flyer' passing Old Oak on 9 October 1965.
G M Cashmore/*The Railway Magazine *Archives.

RIGHT: The 'Panda Pullman' waiting to depart Paddington with a five coach train on Saturday 13 November 1965.
Brian Stephenson/*The Railway Magazine *Archives.

7
6
5
4
3
TICKET OFFICE
SUBWAY
PANDA
PULLMAN
Nº 4472

During the heady days which followed No.4472's preservation by Alan Pegler, the locomotive visited many different locations around the country, however, as BR progressively withdrew facilities for servicing steam locomotives, coaling and watering facilities became increasingly rare, a situation which started to cause some anxious moments. Initially, these problems were overcome by the formation of a small group of volunteers - with the name Flying Scotsman Enterprises - who took on the task of making No.4472 a completely self-contained unit regarding maintenance and servicing. Several contractors also joined the organisation, their responsibilities being to supply the coal by lorry and water by road tanker at whatever location it was required.

Back in 1928, No.4472 had been the first locomotive in the world to be equipped with a corridor tender and when Alan Pegler purchased the locomotive in 1963, he had arranged that the standard tender attached to *Flying Scotsman*, be exchanged with the corridor tender from A4 No.60034. Because of the advantages associated with the corridor tender and because of their increasing rarity, in early 1966 Alan Pegler arranged to purchase for under £1000 the corridor tender from A4 No.60009 *Union of South Africa*, not for coal but to carry an extra 6000 gallons of water. After another £5000 had been spent on the conversion and for ensuring that the tender could operate safely at speeds up to 80 mph, *Flying Scotsman* first emerged from Doncaster with two tenders on 3 October 1966. At the same time, the LNER crests on the cab sides were restored, the normal tender carrying the initials L.N.E.R. and the second tender 4472.

LEFT: One of the more unusual locations visited during the mid-1960s was Brighton, No.4472 pictured after hauling a special from London Victoria to Brighton and Eastleigh on 17 September 1966. From Brighton, No.4472 took its train to Preston Park, Hove, Havant, Southampton and then Eastleigh where the locomotive was serviced. From Eastleigh, a pair of Standard 4MT tanks covered the trip to Salisbury and return. ***John Bird/*****The Railway Magazine** ***Archives.***

ABOVE: The fans turn out to see *Flying Scotsman* on its first revenue-earning run with two tenders on 8 October 1966. The special - the GMRS 'Blackpool Belle' - is pictured at Hebden Bridge just outside Halifax with an illuminations special from Lincoln, the trip including a ride on a tram after arriving at Blackpool North station.
Brian Lister/**The Railway Magazine** ***Archives.***

During 1967 and 1968 *Flying Scotsman* made several historic trips to East Anglia. These were important because firstly, they were the first excursions made under Alan Pegler's exclusive contract to run No.4472 on BR tracks at that time (all other steam locomotives were barred). Secondly, Gresley Pacifics had always been denied access to East Anglia because of weight restrictions. However, the most important event of 1967 took place on Saturday 17 June. Forty years previously, the LNER had inaugurated the first non-stop service between King's Cross and Newcastle with a train hauled by Gresley Pacific *Flying Fox*. To commemorate this notable event, Alan Pegler's *Flying Scotsman* would haul a special train - 'The Hadrian Flyer' - over the same route, the objective being to perform the King's Cross-Newcastle stage without a stop.

A distinct air of optimism present before the start, the first target on leaving the terminus at 08.14 was to gain a couple of minutes by Hitchin, but because of frequent bouts of slipping in the tunnels leading out of King's Cross - and a speed restriction - Hitchin was passed late rather than early. From that point, time was steadily regained by a fast run to Peterborough, the maximum speed during the journey - 88mph - being clocked beyond Hougham, to be followed at Newark by a prolonged slowing after adverse signals had been sighted. Despite the fireman dropping off the footplate to warn the signalman of the nature of the train, all was lost and the train was brought to a dead stop. A total of 37¼ minutes having been spent astride milepost 131, No.4472 eventually reached Newcastle 32 minutes late, but at a credible average speed in excess of 60mph.

LEFT: 1967 saw No.4472 continuing its tour of Britain and on Sunday 21 May, Alan Pegler proudly poses in front of *Flying Scotsman* which was about to haul the northbound leg of the GMRS 'The Retford Rover' excursion from King's Cross via Stevenage to Retford. *D E Canning.*

RIGHT: No.4472 makes an impressive sight climbing Holloway Bank with the 'Hadrian Flyer' on Saturday 17 June 1967.
Brian Stephenson/*The Railway Magazine *Archives.

THE HADRIAN FLYER
No 4472
LNER

On 1 May 1968, an event occurred involving No.4472 *Flying Scotsman* that brought to life memories of an achievement that had occurred exactly 40 years previously. On 1 May 1928, No.4472 had hauled the first non-stop 'Flying Scotsman' train between King's Cross-Edinburgh (392.7 miles) in eight hours three minutes. Forty years later, Alan Pegler was attempting to repeat this performance, although in vastly changed circumstances. With steam traction virtually at an end on British Railways, it was not enough to have a locomotive of suitable calibre available, also required was the certainty of having enough coal and water to complete the journey non-stop, as well as having the enginemen who could undertake such a task.

Nevertheless, through the enthusiasm and enterprise of Alan Pegler, the support of the LCGB and the whole-hearted co-operation of BR, the 40th Anniversary was celebrated satisfactorily with a non-stop run, *Flying Scotsman* with a seven-coach train entering Edinburgh's Waverley station 7¾ hours after leaving King's Cross without the wheels having stopped turning - but only just! Despite the extra 6000 gallons carried in the second tender, the overriding problem was still that of water supply and there were several anxious moments during the journey because of poor 'fill-ups' at the remaining water troughs along the route.

From start to finish, *Flying Scotsman's* progress was the subject of much attention, with every vantage point packed along the route and helicopters carrying BBC Television cameras frequently passed over the train, recording every moment of this historic anniversary run. As No.4472 left from Platform 10 at King's Cross, simultaneously at 10.00, the 'Flying Scotsman' train - hauled by Deltic No.D9021 *Argyle and Sutherland Highlander* - also left, which, despite a stop at Newcastle, reached Edinburgh nearly two hours before the steam-hauled train!

LEFT: With safety valves lifting, No.4472 prepares to leave King's Cross at the start of the 40th Anniversary non-stop run to Edinburgh on 1 May 1968.
***Fox Photos Ltd*/The Railway Magazine *Archives*.**

RIGHT: *Flying Scotsman* passes Newcastle Central and crosses Castle Junction with the 40th Anniversary special. *V C K Allen*/The Railway Magazine.

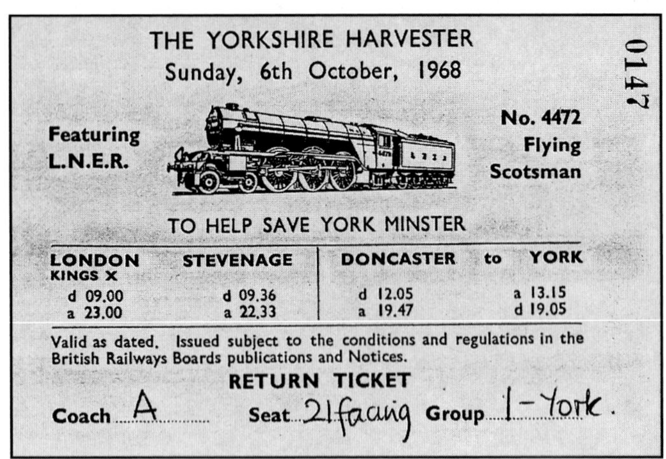

THE YORKSHIRE HARVESTER
Sunday, 6th October, 1968

0147

Featuring L.N.E.R. No. 4472 Flying Scotsman

TO HELP SAVE YORK MINSTER

LONDON KINGS X	STEVENAGE	DONCASTER	to	YORK
d 09.00	d 09.36	d 12.05		a 13.15
a 23.00	a 22.33	a 19.47		d 19.05

Valid as dated. Issued subject to the conditions and regulations in the British Railways Boards publications and Notices.

RETURN TICKET

Coach A Seat 21 facing Group 1 - York.

ABOVE: After August 1968, No.4472 was the only steam locomotive permitted to operate over standard-gauge tracks on the BR network and on this occasion is pictured at the head of the 'Yorkshire Harvester' which ran between King's Cross and York on Sunday 6 October 1968. ***Norman E Preedy.***

LEFT: On Saturday 25 May 1968, *Flying Scotsman* took the 'Forth Bridge Flyer' from Stockton-on-Tees to Edinburgh, then over the Forth Bridge and return. With the imminent total demise of steam, the special was advertised as 'almost certainly the last opportunity to travel steam hauled over the Forth Bridge' and No.4472 is illustrated at North Queensferry, prior to turning at Inverkeithing for the return journey.
T G Hepburn/**The Railway Magazine** ***Archives.***

In 1968, it was proposed that *Flying Scotsman* be sent to North America at the head of a British Trade Mission, an idea which arose because of the celebrity status of No.4472 in the United States at that time. There were several precedents, locomotives from Great Britain having been sent to America as ambassadors in 1893, 1927, 1933 and 1939.

While the details of the 2000 mile sales promotion trip were firmed up, in preparation for the visit, in November 1968, No.4472 entered the Hunslet Engine Works at Leeds for heavy overhaul, which would include a complete boiler retube. In addition, an American bell and whistle were fitted, although the latter would be replaced by a chime whistle in the USA.

As the overhaul progressed, the locomotive was inspected by officials from the US Transport Commission and Canadian National Railways who found *Flying Scotsman* to be 'totally sound and of superior workmanship to our own requirements in some departments'.

RIGHT: With the major overhaul of No.4472 already well underway, the boiler of Festiniog Railway 0-4-0 saddle-tank tender locomotive *Linda* is unloaded from a lorry at the Hunslet Engine Works, Leeds on 11 November 1968.
The Railway Magazine *Archives*.

LEFT: The date for the North American adventure being delayed for various reasons, No.4472 continued to be used for railtours and typical of the welcome that Alan Pegler's preserved A3 was to receive in every location visited, was that at Barnsley, where most of the population appeared to have turned out to welcome No.4472 to Exchange station. No wonder, *Flying Scotsman* was a welcome sight, bringing some cheer to the immediate post-steam and post-Beeching era after arriving with a railtour on 21 June 1969. The train had travelled from Manchester via Woodhead being hauled through the tunnel by an electric locomotive with 'Scottie' in light steam. ***A J Booth.***

Meanwhile, the arrangements for *Flying Scotsman's* visit to North America with a British Trade mission were being finalised. Because fitting-out work on some of the vehicles forming the nine-coach exhibition train had been carried out there, Twickenham station in Middlesex became the unlikely starting point for the trans-Atlantic journey, No.4472 on 18 August, working a train of four coaches from Twickenham to Liverpool for loading on board ship. In addition, a further four coaches were worked separately to Liverpool.

On Sunday 31 August, No.4472 worked its last railtour over BR metals and on 14 September ran with both tenders and one carriage from Doncaster to Edge Hill, Liverpool.

RIGHT: On 19 September the massive floating crane *Mammoth* carefully lifted the A3 high above Brocklebank East Dock, Liverpool *en route* to the deck of the Cunard Line's *Saxonia* and the United States of America and Canada. Safely on board, Alan Pegler ceremoniously launched the North American tour by breaking a bottle of champagne over No.4472's buffer-beam. ***J R Hillier*/The Railway Magazine *Archives*.**

ABOVE: After a 10-day, 3,500 mile ocean voyage, on 28 September, the *Saxonia* was manouevred into position in the middle of Boston Harbour to allow large floating cranes to unload No.4472, its two tenders and two cars onto the quayside at the Boston Army Base. Joining the seven other vehicles forming the Exhibition train (which had arrived by earlier sailings), the whole train was assembled for a trial run over Penn Central tracks on 3 October, before going on exhibition at Boston's South station later the same day. *Paul Huntington/Allan Richardson.*

ABOVE: On a drizzly Sunday 12 October 1969, No.4472 left Boston's South station at the commencement of its official tour of North America and during the next few weeks, the A3 visited many towns and cities with the Exhibition train. However, the highlight of this first stage of the tour, would take place on Sunday 2 November, at the medium-sized Alabama city of Anniston, when three preserved steam locomotives - one British and two American - met up. Crowds estimated at between 3-5000 people turned up to witness the historic occasion, which took place during the Southern Railway's 75th Anniversary year.
Allan Richardson.

After touring the US during June-July 1970, *Flying Scotsman* ran up the middle of the USA south to north from Texas to Wisconsin, terminating at the National Rail Road Museum at Green Bay on 19 July, where the Pullman Car *Isle of Thanet* was delivered (one of the reasons for the 1970 tour) to join other British exhibits, including Gresley A4 Pacific *Dwight D Eisenhower*. From Green Bay, travelling by night for the first time in the USA, No.4472 ran via Chicago, entering Canada on 20 August and crossing the international boundary below ground level and below the waters of the St Clair River via the St Clair tunnel at Sarnia, Ontario.

After spending 10 days on exhibition at the Canadian National Exhibition at Toronto in September, No.4472 then undertook tours to Ottawa, Montreal and Kingston. After this minor tour, in preparation for the severe Canadian winter, *Flying Scotsman* returned its train to Toronto, the locomotive being stored under cover in Spadina Roundhouse. The Exhibition train fared less well, being stored in the open, a period of snow wreaking havoc with paintwork and with the interiors becoming vulnerable to badly leaking roofs.

LEFT: On 21 August, No.4472 ran from Sarnia to Toronto for display for 10 days at the Canadian National Exhibition and is pictured here after easing away from Burlington, Ontario, through a temporary speed restriction *en route* to Toronto. The two white flags carried on the buffer beam indicated that the train was a 'special' carrying passengers/exhibitors.
Patricia J Brown/Gresley Society Collection.

RIGHT: On 28 August 1970, No.4472 poses at Spadina Roundhouse, Toronto, alongside CN 4-8-4 No.6218, the only operational CN steam locomotive.
James A Brown/Gresley Society Collection.

L N E R
6218
CN
6218
6218
44 72

With rumours of financial problems casting doubt over *Flying Scotsman* being able to continue its tour of North America, in an attempt to save the venture, the decision was made to move the train to San Francisco. Consequently, on 27 September 1971, No.4472 with the Exhibition train - after a trans-continental journey - was ferried across San Francisco Bay to Fisherman's Wharf, there going on display for four months. In March the following year, an attempt was made to upstage San Francisco's famous cable cars by using No.4472 to operate a passenger service at weekends along a two-mile section of the Belt Railway, the system of tracks which served the port area. However, this attempt was doomed to failure and soon abandoned. The final nail in the coffin was hammered home after complaints about the locomotive's presence at Fisherman's Wharf, forced the train to move to a less accessible site, which brought a considerable reduction in the number of visitors. With the future uncertain, on 12 August the A3 and the Exhibition train were once again ferried back across the Bay to Oakland, in readiness for a short excursion the following day to Stockton, from where No.4472 - in light steam but diesel hauled - would work to the US Army's Sharpe Depot at Lathrop, California for winter storage.

ABOVE: No.4472 pictured at Fisherman's Wharf, San Francisco in the winter of 1971. Clearly illustrated in this photograph is the extra equipment required before *Flying Scotsman* was allowed to operate over the North American railway network.
C W R Bowman/Gresley Society Collection.

On the other side of the Atlantic, disturbing reports that Alan Pegler was experiencing financial difficulties, spurred action from several quarters. As it became evident that *Flying Scotsman* and its train was at risk of being seized by creditors and sold to recover at least part of the outstanding debt, a member of a leading British construction company and well-known railway enthusiast - 'Mr Bill' McAlpine - stepped in to save the day. Negotiations completed with the known creditors and with ownership of the locomotive now transferred to Mr McAlpine, hurried arrangements were made for the return of the locomotive to the United Kingdom, lest some previously unheard of creditor should surface and block the move. From storage at the Sharpe Army Base, No.4472 - after being surreptitiously moved to Oakland docks on 19 January 1973 - was loaded on board the MV *California Star* on 22 January, the ship sailing the same night.

ABOVE: Travelling via the Panama Canal, the *California Star* - with the locomotive and two tenders secured firmly to the deck - was forced to brave the full force of an Atlantic gale, before arriving at Seaforth, Liverpool on the evening of Tuesday 13 February, the ship moving to Gladstone Dock for unloading on Wednesday 14 February. The effects of this severe weather is clearly illustrated in this photograph as the snow-covered locomotive and tenders are prepared for unloading. *John Buckley.*

RIGHT: Almost there! To the delight of steam enthusiasts everywhere, No.4472 is in sight of being repatriated, the famous Pacific really 'flying', lifted once again by the floating crane *Mammoth* from the deck of the *California Star* under a darkening winter sky. *John Buckley.*

After refurbishment at the Derby Works of BREL, No.4472 was outshopped with black-backed nameplates, black cylinder side casings and with cabside numbers restored and on 15 July 1973, resplendent in new Apple-Green livery, travelled under its own steam to Paignton for a 10-week season on the Torbay Steam Railway.

RIGHT: With the busy town of Dartmouth on the west side of the River Dart and Kingswear on the east bank forming an interesting backcloth, No.4472 running tender first, returns a service train to Paignton on 24 August 1973. *Gavin W Morrison.*

Quickly spruced up and already devoid of some of the American trappings, No.4472 was passed fit to travel under its own steam and with both tenders, to the Derby Works of British Rail Engineering Ltd, for light repair and repainting. Making good use of the full tender of Utah coal which returned with the locomotive, No.4472 on its first journey over British metals since the summer of 1969, stole the hearts of the many spectators that gathered all along the route to welcome home Britain's most reluctant emigrant.

At a ceremony held at Derby on 14 July 1973, another chapter in the life of the 'world's most famous locomotive' was launched, the Right Hon Richard Marsh (Chairman of British Rail) handing over the refurbished locomotive to the new owner Mr McAlpine. From Derby, the A3 moved south, heading for the Torbay Steam Railway.

ABOVE: A few days after returning from North America, No.4472 looks in fine fettle on Monday 19 February, passing through Broad Green after leaving Edge Hill Depot *en route* to the BREL Works at Derby. Despite the significance of the occasion, the approaching 'official' appears completely oblivious of the event! *John Buckley.*

RIGHT: The man who made it all possible, the Hon William McAlpine ('Mr Bill' to many who knew him) who later became Sir William McAlpine Bt, receiving the hereditary title of his father, who died on 7 January 1990.

4472
L N E R

No.4472 remained in Devon until 18 September 1973, the A3 then being prepared for its first commercial run over BR tracks since returning from the USA. This was the 'Atlantic Venturers Express', *Flying Scotsman* and GWR No.6000 *King George V* - both locomotives now having visited North America - double-heading a 15-coach special between Newport, Hereford and Shrewsbury. The order of running was decided by the Mayor of Newport tossing a coin, with the winner (No.4472) leading from Newport-Hereford and the loser (No.6000) from Hereford-Shrewsbury.

ABOVE: In pouring rain, No.4472 pilots *KGV* on the first leg of the journey near Llanvihangel Summit on 22 September 1973. *Gavin W Morrison*.

Now under the ownership of Mr McAlpine, No.4472's first home depot was a former British Steel ironstone railway depot at Market Overton, the locomotive renewing its acquantance with privately preserved GWR No.4079 *Pendennis Castle* which was also based there. However, with rail access to the depot under threat, the decision was made to move both No.4472 and No.4079 to Steamtown, Carnforth, the A3 arriving at its new base on 10 August 1974.

ABOVE: 1975 saw the Stockton & Darlington 150 Anniversary celebrations, No.4472 in company with many famous as well as lesser known locomotives taking part. With unsteamable NER Fletcher 2-4-0 No.910 hauled dead behind the corridor tender, *Flying Scotsman* was a highlight of the Grand Steam Calvalcade which took place between Shildon and Heighington on the Darlington-Bishop Auckland line on Sunday 31 August. *Gavin W Morrison.*

1976 saw the Centenary of the opening of the Settle & Carlisle route, or the 'Long Drag' as it is sometimes known. To celebrate the event, it was planned to run a 'Centenary Special' on 1 May hauled by Midland 'Compound' 4-4-0 No.1000 and 'Black Five' No.44871. However, due to the unavailability of both locomotives, the unlikely combination of No.4472 *Flying Scotsman* (on loan to the National Railway Museum at York at the time) and LNWR 'Precedent' 2-4-0 No.790 *Hardwicke* were substituted on the train of historic saloons which ran in the morning of May Day 1976.

ABOVE: During 1976, 4-6-0 No.1306 *Mayflower*, No.4472 *Flying Scotsman* and No.790 *Hardwicke* were all active from Carnforth over the erstwhile Furness Railway and in this photograph taken on 8 May, *Hardwicke* pilots No.4472 across the viaduct over the Leven Estuary.
Gavin W Morrison.

One of many such enterprises which occurred during the ownership of *Flying Scotsman* by the Hon 'Bill' McAlpine occurred on 25 July 1976, when the biggest promotional exhibition claimed ever to have been mounted on the British railway network was inaugurated at a ceremony held at Leeds station, the Shriro (UK) Ltd 'Pioneer Express' (promoting Pioneer Hi-Fi equipment) travelling from Carnforth to Leeds hauled by No.4472 *Flying Scotsman*. The train consisting of a service car, club car, three exhibition cars, generator/brake van and brake/stores van had been fitted out at Kensington Olympia, shown to the press at Marylebone on 22 July and worked to Carnforth overnight on the 23/24 July, the train leaving Leeds on the first leg of its journey at 15.00 on 25 July. All the vehicles had been refurbished internally and painted externally white with the Pioneer *motif* in blue. Wherever possible, the 'Pioneer Express' was steam hauled, visits taking place at locations right across the country. In August, the 'Pioneer Express' visited Kingswear in Devon via the Torbay Steam Railway, but a visit to Minehead via the West Somerset Railway had to be changed to Exeter following a dispute with the local branch of the National Union of Railwaymen.

ABOVE: The 'Pioneer Express' photographed between Leeds and Shipley on 25 July 1976. *Tom Heavyside.*

ABOVE: The disappearance of the author Agatha Christie in 1926 to a secret hideout in a Harrogate hotel, prompted a film about the mysterious event. One of the stars of the film was *Flying Scotsman* with the A3 playing a double role with the nameplate and number of No.4474 *Victor Wild* on one side and No.4480 *Enterprise* on the other! Captured on 27 November 1977, No.4472 masquerades as No.4474 *en route* from Carnforth to York (which doubled as Harrogate station) for the filming of 'Agatha'. *Les Nixon*.

A month later on 16 December, *Flying Scotsman* entered Vickers Works at Barrow-in-Furness for major overhaul, being outshopped six months later on 6 June 1978, the locomotive returning to its base at Carnforth the same day. On 15 June, No.4472 took an eight-coach train of mostly preserved stock from Carnforth across the Ribblehead Viaduct to Carlisle, this stock forming a *Flying Scotsman* hauled special the following day - 16 June - from Carlisle to Hellifield for owner Mr 'Bill' McAlpine. From Hellifield, No.4472 continued with one coach to Keighley, where GNR 'Atlantic' No.990 *Henry Oakley* and a brake van were collected and taken via Leeds to Doncaster for 'Railex 125', Doncaster Works 125 Anniversary celebrations that weekend.

ABOVE: No.4472 takes water from a road tanker at Long Preston on Friday 16 June 1978. *Gavin W Morrison.*

The last day of September 1978 was the occasion for a remarkable tribute to railway enthusiast Right Revd Eric Treacy who died from a heart attack on the platform at Appleby station on Saturday 13 May 1978, having gone there to see and photograph BR 9F class 2-10-0 No.92220 *Evening Star*. As a memorial and tribute to Eric Treacy, BR London Midland Region under the direction of steam supremo David Ward organised two steam hauled specials, the 'Lord Bishop' which ran on Saturday 30 September from London, Euston to Appleby with a stop at Hellifield where the diesel locomotive was exchanged for a specially spruced up *Flying Scotsman*. A second train - the 'Bishop Treacy' - ran via the Settle & Carlisle from Halifax to Appleby enabling former parishioners of the late Bishop and churchmen to attend a memorial service which was held in the town. At Appleby, to the south of the railway station, an open space had been cleared, 4000 people attending a moving and unusual memorial, with the start and finish of a minute's silence being announced by the sounding of *Evening Star's* whistle, the locomotive serving as a background during the service.

ABOVE: *Flying Scotsman* crosses the Ribblehead Viaduct on the Settle & Carlisle line on Saturday 30 September 1978.
Gavin W Morrison.

1979 would be a busy year for Bill McAlpine's A3 and with the programme of BR promoted steam excursions accelerating, the London Midland Region announced that following the success of the 1978 BR sponsored steam/diesel hauled trains between Blackpool and Sellafield - the 'Cumbrian Coast Express' - the programme for 1979 would be expanded by increasing the number of days on which the 'CCE' ran and by adding a new scenic excursion. This new train was named the 'North Yorkshireman' and would be worked by four locomotives from the Carnforth stud, including No.4472. Meanwhile, the Eastern Region confirmed that in 1979, the York circular tour - the precursor of the 'Scarborough Spa Express' - would operate again, the tour covering the same route as the previous year - York-Church Fenton-Leeds-Harrogate-York. Again, No.4472 was one of a fleet of five locomotives diagrammed to haul these excursions. In addition, No.4472 also featured in the SLOA steam programme, being used between York and Carlisle on several specials run over the S&C - namely 'The Northumbrian Limited' and 'The Hadrian Limited', as well as the final main steam trip of the year, the 29 December 'Santa Special', No.4472 working from Carnforth-Sellafield and *Sir Nigel Gresley* returning the train to Carnforth.

Flying Scotsman started the new decade by being chosen as one of the locomotives diagrammed for a programme of Winter steam excursions on the Settle & Carlisle line, the SLOA 'Cumbrian Mountain Express'. Initially, six 'CMEs' were proposed for the months of January, February and March, running alternately north and south between Skipton and Carlisle. So great was the demand, a further six trains had to be organised and in the event, over 5000 passengers were carried over the S&C during the first four months of 1980.

LEFT: On Sunday 17 June 1979, with the mechanical ash-disposal tower in the background, Erica Arneil (a Steamtown volunteer) removes ashes from the smokebox of No.4472, the locomotive standing on the ash-disposal road at Carnforth. *Flying Scotsman* had just returned from the main line, having taken the northbound leg of a Leeds-Carnforth railtour - 'The Lancastrian' - the train being returned southbound by No.4498 *Sir Nigel Gresley*.
Tom Heavyside.

RIGHT: A wintry scene, with patches of snow evident on the backcloth of hills behind as No.4472 - photographed heading north on the S&C - crosses Arten Gill Viaduct on Saturday 29 March 1980.
Gavin W Morrison.

1980 bore testimony to the success of two pioneering railway projects in Britain 150 years previously. The first of these took place in May at Canterbury in connection with the 150th Anniversary of the Canterbury & Whitstable Railway. However, pride of place would fall to the Anniversary celebrations of the Liverpool & Manchester Railway. On 12 March 1980, No.4472 hauled a Post Office philatelic special from Liverpool (Lime Street) to Manchester (Victoria) on the first day of issue of special commemorative Liverpool & Manchester 150 postage stamps. In addition, No.4472 appeared in a cavalcade of locomotives which took place at Rainhill on 24-26 March.

The summer of 1981 saw the first of a series of BR Eastern Region operated excursions from York to Scarborough and back, the inaugural 'Scarborough Spa Express' on 25 May coinciding with the official re-opening of the Spa after extensive renovation. The operation of the 'SSE' - which operated on Tuesdays from 14 July-1 September - had been made possible by the installation of the former Gateshead depot 60ft turntable in the original turntable pit at Seamer Road, Scarborough. A few days before the first train ran - 23 May - an urgent call from BR York to Steamtown, Carnforth requested a locomotive to replace failed *Duchess of Hamilton*, No.4472 being promptly prepared and despatched to work the train.

LEFT: On a wet August Tuesday in 1980, Nos.5407 and 4472 climb out of Bolton over mean streets and damp cobbles reminiscent of another era, *en route* to Carnforth.
Bob Avery.

RIGHT: On home ground under the cavernous roof of York station, No.4472 prepares to leave with the 29 July 1981 'Scarborough Spa Express'.
Chris Milner.

4472
302
522

1982 would see *Flying Scotsman* temporarily lose its tender, the A3 running for the next two years with A4 No.4498's corridor tender in green livery and with raised silver LNER letters, while a new body was made for the A3's tender chassis. During the Summer of 1982, the 'Cumbrian Coast Express' ran again and No.4472's usual role during this period was taking the 10-coach 'CCE' from its Carnforth Depot along the coast of Morecombe Bay.

In 1983, *Flying Scotsman* commenced its Diamond Jubilee year still based at Steamtown, Carnforth the Museum taking the opportunity to sell suitable souvenirs etc. In addition, a 'Flying Scotsman Jubilee' Exhibition was held which consisted of models, paintings and other items of interest. On 30 January 1983, No.4472 worked a private charter train in almost blizzard conditions, a SLOA Annual General Meeting special - 'The Queen of Scots' - from Carlisle to Appleby via the S&C.

LEFT: With the Leven Estuary in the background, No.4472 makes a fine sight, as with white exhaust trailing the whole length of the train and even beyond, the A3 makes light work of hauling the ex-Carnforth 'Santa Steam Pullman' near Plumpton Junction on 28 December 1982.
D Trevor Rowe.

RIGHT: The photograph speaks for itself - the appalling conditions at Garsdale on 30 January 1983, was not enough to deter the intrepid fans of *Flying Scotsman* who were determined to see and photograph No.4472 on the SLOA AGM special 'The Queen of Scots'.
Gavin W Morrison.

THE
QUEEN OF SCOTS
No 4472

DIAMOND JUBILEE
FLYING SCOTSMAN
4472
Nº 4472

On Thursday 24 February 1983, No.4472 found itself taking a back seat while the speeches were made at its own birthday party at Carnforth, before later the same day, complete with commemorative headboard, working the steam leg between Carnforth and York and return of the first SLOA 'Diamond Jubilee' railtour from Crewe. The following day - 25 February, the A3 went on display at the NRM and on 26 February ran light to Doncaster where the locomotive was displayed with other exhibits from Steamtown in readiness for the second SLOA 'Diamond Jubilee' train on Sunday 27 February from London King's Cross, with No.4472 taking the train over the ECML from Peterborough (electrification preventing the use of the section from King's Cross) to York via Normanton. The event was marred, however, by the irresponsible behaviour of photographers, particularly near Stoke Bank.

Also in 1983, an unusual association was formed between *Flying Scotsman* and the Parachute Regiment. At the time, the CO (Edward Gardener) of the 15th (Scottish Volunteer) Battalion (15 PARA), a TA unit based in Glasgow suggested an association between the locomotive and 15 PARA, the proposal being readily taken up by owner Bill McAlpine. The Battalion had a specialist mobilisation role in urban warfare and as it was important that the soldiers experienced basic railway operation, training sessions were arranged at Carnforth.

LEFT: To surprisingly deserted platforms, No.4472 passes through Keighley station with the 24 February 1983 'Diamond Jubilee' special. The raised letters on the A4 tender can be clearly seen in this photograph.
Gavin W Morrison.

RIGHT: Sunday 4 September 1983 saw the CO of 15 PARA at the controls of *Flying Scotsman,* other members of the Regiment standing guard as the locomotive moved around its Carnforth base. Later in the day, a ceremony took place commemorating the adoption of the locomotive by the Parachute Regiment, small brass plaques being presented, which were then mounted on the locomotive's splashers.
Edward Gardener Collection.

FLYING SCOTSMAN

SOUVENIR
TICKET

VISIT BY No. 4472 "FLYING SCOTSMAN"
IN HER DIAMOND JUBILEE YEAR
TO GLASGOW QUEEN STREET STATION

In Association with the

15th (SCOTTISH VOLUNTEER) BATTALION
THE PARACHUTE REGIMENT

2nd OCT '83 25p

Continuing their supporting role, 15 PARA's next major contact with *Flying Scotsman* was during the locomotive's visit to Scotland in the Autumn of 1983, a special Battalion headboard being carried throughout. During the visit North of the Border, No.4472 was based at Eastfield MPD at Glasgow, 15 PARA re-inforcing the support crew and even providing a round-the-clock guard against vandals. On 1 October, the A3 hauled a special - 'The Fair Maid' - to Stirling, Perth and Edinburgh via the Forth Bridge. The following day, the locomotive went on public display at Glasgow Queen Street, supervised by the Battalion, who also set up a recruiting stand! On the last day, No.4472 was the major attraction at a McAlpine Trade Exhibition at Edinburgh Waverley where again, 15 PARA provided support, one of the Unit's pipers composing a special tune in *Flying Scotsman's* honour.

One of the many highlights of *Flying Scotsman's* long career took place on Tuesday 20 November 1984, when No.4472 was rostered to haul the Royal Train carrying HRH The Queen Mother between Stratford Low Level and North Woolwich in East London to open the new North Woolwich Station Museum. Resplendent after the combined exertions of a team of 12 people, No.4472 - right down to chevroned buffers and white-painted vacuum hoses - looked the part, highlighted still further by the glistening white cab roof, a symbol of former GER Royal Train practice. On arrival at North Woolwich, the Queen Mother - who travelled in SLOA Pullman Car No.351 - unveiled an oval brass plaque to commemorate the event, in addition to mounting the footplate of No.4472.

ABOVE: Still in ex-Royal Train condition, No.4472 is pictured at Sheffield on a SLOA King's Cross-Manchester steam railtour on Saturday 24 November 1984. *D Trevor Rowe.*

OPPOSITE PAGE: No.4472 climbing to the Forth Bridge from Inverkeithing on 1 October 1983 with 'The Fair Maid' on the Perth-Edinburgh leg . *Tom Heavyside.*

Between March-27 December 1985, *Flying Scotsman* underwent a major overhaul at Carnforth and at this time, a new person to take charge of the locomotive's maintenance was being sought by owner Bill McAlpine.

With a background in engineering from the age of 16, Roland Kennington agreed to take on this responsibility, becoming as time went on, almost synonymous with the name *Flying Scotsman* itself. Roland took up his duties in December 1985, when No.4472 moved to a new base at Marylebone, London to take up duties on the Sunday 'Shakespeare Limited' London to Stratford-upon-Avon luncheon trains. The following year - 1986 - *Flying Scotsman* had no less than 32 outings on the main line, clearly a busy period for the new CME.

However, it was 1988 which proved a watershed year for Roland. The Australian tour was arranged and he was asked to go with it, 28,000 miles being covered without a single incident of the locomotive having to be failed because of mechanical problems.

After overseeing the overhaul of *Flying Scotsman* at Babcock Robey in April-July 1993, Roland continued - with the help of a small group of dedicated volunteers - to look after the locomotive, finally becoming Chief Engineer of Flying Scotsman Railways Ltd upon the purchase of No.4472 by Dr Tony Marchington in February 1996.

LEFT: Roland Kennington in the cab of No.4472.

RIGHT: Sharing the day's duties on the 'Shakespeare Limited' on Sunday 26 October 1986 with A4 No.4468 *Mallard* (which took the first train of the day), No.4472 *Flying Scotsman* makes a spirited start from Marylebone. On this occasion No.35028 *Clan Line* was the stand-by locomotive. *Brian Morrison.*

In 1988, the celebration of Australia's Bi-Centennial Year brought together a group of like-minded people who were convinced that a railway display should form a principal part of the celebrations, because of the importance of the 'iron road' in the development of Australia as a nation. Melbourne, No.4472's first destination in Australia, has two railway gauges (standard 4ft 8½in. and broad 5ft 3in.), New South Wales has an extensive standard gauge system, Brisbane and Perth have both standard and narrow gauge and Adelaide standard and broad gauge. Thus it was possible to visit all of these major cities. Additionally, as Australia's first railway locomotives had come from Britain, it was felt to be essential that a British locomotive also take part. After various enquiries had been made, owner Bill McAlpine agreed that *Flying Scotsman* could be released, but only after cast-iron financial guarantees had been received about funding and for transporting the locomotive to the other side of the world and back.

As a prelude to the Australian adventure, on 27 February 1988, No.4472 hauled a charter special to West Ruislip, the locomotive then running to Southall Depot in West London for stripping to enable the

LEFT: Photographed from the bridge of the *New Zealand Pacific* in the evening of Sunday 11 September, No.4472 and tender is shown securely fastened to the ship's deck, ready for the five-week sea journey to Sydney via the Cape of Good Hope. Note that the chimney is covered to prevent rain and seawater entering the smokebox and steam chests. In the early morning of the 12 September, the ship sailed for Sydney. *Ken Brunt.*

driving wheels to be removed for retyring and for major mechanical repairs to be undertaken. Rebuilding completed, steam was raised for the first time on Sunday 7 August and after satisfactory test runs, No.4472 on Sunday 21 August - without lettering or lining - successfully hauled the Up 'Shakespeare' luncheon train express from Stratford to Marylebone. On 2 September, the locomotive emerged resplendent from Southall Depot in freshly applied Apple-Green livery and with lettering and lining completed.

Final preparations made, on 11 September No.4472 was brought to the railhead of Tilbury Container Services by BR's 'Railfreight' locomotive No.37-358 *P&O Containers*, the A3 then being winched on to a multi-axle road trailer for the short journey to the quayside. A floating crane - the *London Samson* - then lifted the 85½-ton locomotive onto a heavy-duty platform fitted with rails and sleepers (completely surrounded by containers for maximum protection against the sea and weather during the long voyage) on the deck of the container ship *New Zealand Pacific*.

Flying Scotsman arrived at the Port of Melbourne on 11 October 1988, where it was inspected, the ship then sailing to Sydney for unloading, as Melbourne did not have a crane large enough.

RIGHT: On 16 October 1988, poised precariously over Sydney Harbour, No.4472 dangles from the arm of a floating crane, the long sea journey completed and a gruelling 28,000 mile trans-continental tour across Australia ahead.

After unloading at Sydney, *Flying Scotsman* was towed from the quayside by State Rail Authority of NSW 44 Class Locomotive No.4472 to Eveleigh Workshops, where - less than 36 hours after being unloaded from the *New Zealand Pacific* - the A3 was prepared for a trial run to Wollongong. Very soon after its arrival, *Flying Scotsman* was transferred south to Melbourne, Victoria to take part in the Aus Steam '88 celebrations and during the lengthy stay hauled numerous special excursions to Seymour and return. When not being used on special trains, the locomotive was put on display inside a specially constructed compound at Spencer Street station.

After a very successful season in Victoria, No.4472 then moved north to New South Wales, where the standard gauge system offered a great deal more variety for tours and the opportunity was taken to visit as many towns and cities as possible. During its stay, the A3 was normally based in Sydney, but it did include Brisbane, Dubbo and Moss Vale on its agenda. The rapturous response which greeted *Flying Scotsman* during all the stages of the Australia tour are clearly illustrated in these two photographs.

ABOVE: On arrival at Albury on the NSW/Victoria state boundary from Melbourne on 25 October 1988, No.4472 comes off the train to go for servicing.
Hugh Ballantyne.

LEFT: No.4472 stands on Dapto's Loop platform after arriving from Sydney on 19 February 1989. ***J Costigan.***

OPPOSITE PAGE: The first public run of No.4472 during its highly successful tour of Australia took place on 25 October 1988, the A3 photographed crossing the lofty Maribyrnong Viaduct a few miles north of Melbourne *en route* over the Victoria standard gauge line from Melbourne to Albury.
Hugh Ballantyne.

4472
L N E R

Flying Scotsman did a lot of its long distance touring in NSW in the company of preserved Class 38 Pacific No.3801. The two locomotives travelled hundreds of kilometres throughout the State and made quite a spectacle climbing grades and speeding through the countryside, the unique three-cylinder beat of the A3 and the sharp bark of the 38 in marked contrast to one another. Over an extended weekend from 9-12 June 1989, the two locomotives visited Dubbo and then did a local return trip to Orange, before returning to Sydney.

As Nos.4472 and 3801 prepared to depart Dubbo in the early morning of 12 June for the long journey back to Sydney, the temperature was just above freezing, the smoke rose in the air and then plateaued before slowly drifting in a westerly direction. As the two locomotives eased their train away from the station, the escaping steam from *Flying Scotsman's* cylinder drain cocks totally obscured the two locomotives (to the annoyance of gathered photographers), it taking over 50 metres for No.4472's smokebox to emerge from the rolling cloud of steam.

After returning to Melbourne for a short time, No.4472 embarked on its legendary tour to Alice Springs on 6 August 1989. As a fitting farewell to Victoria, two R Class locomotives ran on the broad gauge to Seymour with No.4472 on the standard gauge. One thing that the four steam locomotives present had in common (J515 was in steam at Seymour to assist R707 which was returning to Melbourne with its train) - was that all had been built in Britain, Nos.R761 and R707 both products of the North British Locomotive Company of Glasgow, J515 from the Vulcan Foundry and No.4472 from the LNER's Doncaster Workshops.

OPPOSITE PAGE (MAIN PICTURE): Nos.4472 and 3801 were captured on film to the south of Geurie on 12 June, the crisp morning air helping to produce a good steam effect. *Steve McNicol.*

OPPOSITE PAGE (INSET): The almost volcanic eruption as Nos.4472 - with cylinder drain cocks open - and 3801 pull away from Dubbo earlier the same day. *Steve McNicol.*

ABOVE: Before the start of the marathon journey to the baking 'Red Centre' of the island continent, beneath threatening storm clouds, two photo runs were made at Dysart siding, the three locomotives being lined up at Schoolhouse Lane crossing, before storming past assembled photographers on 6 August 1989. *Steve McNicol.*

On Sunday 6 August 1989, No.4472 left Melbourne at the start of its legendary tour to Alice Springs. Leaving Victoria behind, after an overnight servicing stop at Wagga Wagga, No.4472 - taking the Bethungra spiral in its stride - steamed through the wheatfields and sheep-farming country of mid-western NSW, to Parkes. Next day - 8 August - a journey to the 'silver city' of Broken Hill was on the agenda, the A3 in the process setting a new non-stop world record for steam traction, covering the 422 miles 7.59 chains in 9 hours 25 minutes 4.46 seconds with 535 tons gross and resulting in seven different British and Australian drivers getting their hands on the regulator!

After its record-breaking run, No.4472 left Broken Hill for Peterborough, South Australia, to be followed by a run through more exotic countryside towards Port Pirie on the shores of the Spencer Gulf. Continuing to Port Augusta, No.4472 was prepared for its nail-biting journey across the desert to Alice Springs, the A3 becoming the very first steam locomotive ever to use the town's standard gauge terminus (a new 490 mile standard gauge line from Tarcoola had opened in 1980, replacing the previous 3ft 6in. line opened in 1929). *Flying Scotsman* arrived on the outskirts of Alice Springs on 14 August to find half the population of Central Australia waiting to greet it. Later the same day, a series of parallel runs would take place on the two gauges at Lubcke sidings, the only place where the new and old lines met. After its mammoth journey to Alice Springs, *Flying Scotsman* then returned south for a brief visit to Adelaide and was used for several excursions, as well as parallel running with two former South Australian Railways broad gauge steam locomotives - 520 class leader No.520 and 620 class Pacific No.621 - before once again returning to Sydney on 28 August.

LEFT (MAIN PICTURE): Reduced to almost toy like proportions, No.4472 is photographed from the air returning an excursion from Bolivar to Adelaide on 30 August. ***Steve McNicol.***

LEFT (INSET): No.4472 pictured during its epic-making run to Alice Springs on 10 August 1989 near Mingary, SA. ***Steve McNicol.***

ABOVE: On 14 August, No.4472 briefly met former Western Australian Government Railways W class 4-8-2 No.W924 (owned by the Ghan Preservation Society) at Lubcke Siding, the only place the new standard gauge line and a now preserved section of the old 3ft 6in. line run in parallel.
Steve McNicol Collection.

On 28 August, No.4472 left Adelaide, arriving in Sydney on 1 September to be prepared for the very last stage of the Australian adventure - 'The West Australian'. Despite earlier predictions that the reunion to end all reunions might not take place, on 17 September, to the sound of a Highland pipe band, *Flying Scotsman* arrived in Perth in Western Australia. Waiting to greet No.4472 - along with thousands of spectators - was former adversary GWR No.4079 *Pendennis Castle* which had arrived in Perth on 4 September after being transported almost 1000 miles by road from Dampier on the Hamersley Iron Railway, Northern Australia.

To reach Perth, No.4472 crossed the entire 2461 mile Australian continent - from Sydney to Perth via Broken Hill and Port Pirie - and undertook the Nullarbor crossing hauling a load of 780 tons, reaching its destination just nine minutes late! As No.4472 steamed into the East Perth terminal of the standard gauge trans-Australian line, the huge numbers of spectators forced the abandonment of a ceremonial 'kissing of buffers' between the two locomotives, a disappointment more than made up for later. On 24 September - working in harmony - No.4472 piloted No.4079 on a train to Northam, but on the return working as far as West Toodyay, the train ran as two separate workings. In almost a flash-back to the Locomotive Exchanges of 1925, *Flying Scotsman* and *Pendennis Castle* pitched battle with each other on adjacent tracks for a distance of about a kilometre at Avon Yard utilising the main line and the loop line after the two trains had been split. At Toodyay, the two sections combined again to double-head back to Perth.

The exciting interlude over, *Flying Scotsman* steamed back to Sydney for loading aboard the French vessel *La Perouse*, the ship leaving for Tilbury via New Zealand and Cape Horn on 12 November.

TOP: Nos.4472 and 4079 *Pendennis Castle* meet at the standard gauge Perth Terminal station at the completion of *Flying Scotsman's* trip across Australia on 17 September 1989. *Philip Melling.*

BOTTOM: No.4472 pauses with its train on 24 September 1989 at West Toodyay as No.4079 passes watched by some of the local townsfolk. Note the 'Wells Fargo' type coach and horses, dual gauge track and 3ft 6in. gauge workmen's van in the yard. Toodyay is situated at the east end of the Avon Valley, approximately 55 miles from Perth. *Alan Bollans.*

No.4472's return to Britain - its epoch-making and seemingly endless tour of Australia over - was received with much relief from many quarters, as the locomotive was lowered onto British soil on Thursday 14 December after completing the first known circumnavigation of the world by a steam locomotive. Lifted by the same floating crane that had sent the A3 on its Antipodean adventure over 12 months previously, despite wet and windy conditions, No.4472 was eased from the stern end of the ship on to a low-loader at the start of its journey back to Southall for overhaul and to have the air brake and electric lights required 'Down Under' removed.

After a full check-up, *Flying Scotsman's* first main line run in the UK after returning from Australia took place on 2 May 1990. Described as the 'relaunch' of the locomotive in the UK, the 'FSS Executive' was *Flying Scotsman*-hauled on the short stretch from Didcot (where the locomotive had been stabled) to Banbury and return. Before the start of the excursion, once attached to the train at Didcot, No.4472 drew forward to allow Dr John Prideaux of InterCity to unveil a plaque below the nameplate commemorating the fact that: *'On August 8th 1989 this locomotive achieved the world's longest non-stop run for steam traction of 422 miles 7.5 chains between Parkes and Broken Hill in New South Wales, Australia'.*

With No.4472's seven-year main line certificate due to expire on 27 November 1992, *Flying Scotsman* would be in constant use on the main line almost up to the end, the locomotive covering an estimated 12,500 miles since returning from Australia. The end came on 25 October 1992, No.4472 hauling its last main line excursion between Ealing Broadway and Stratford-on-Avon. However, there was still plenty of life in the 'old girl' and with steam heat reconnected, the locomotive commenced what was anticipated would be a lengthy tour of many of Britain's preserved railways.

RIGHT: Looking in remarkably good condition, on a wet and windy winter's day - covered in a protective layer of grease against the sea and elements and complete with name and maker's plate - No.4472 returns to British shores at Tilbury Docks on 14 December 1989. *Brian Morrison.*

4472
L N E R

1993 marked the 70th birthday of *Flying Scotsman* and the year would indeed be a significant one for the locomotive. Between 26 October-1 December 1992, No.4472 had commenced its tour of the country's premier preserved railways with a visit to the Birmingham Railway Museum at Tyseley. This was followed between 3 December 1992-29 January 1993 by a stint at the Great Central Railway at Loughborough. From 31 January-2 March, the locomotive ran on the East Lancashire Railway, in the process attracting record numbers of passengers and with little hint of the serious mechanical problems which would soon become apparent. On 4 March 1993, No.4472 found itself - for the first time - paying a visit to the 5½ mile Llangollen Railway in North Wales, the next stage of its planned tour of preserved railways. Unfortunately, it would be at Llangollen that the tour would stutter to a halt! During a mandatory, pre-steaming inspection, a shattering discovery revealed 29 defective flue tubes as well as other problems leaving no option but to withdraw the locomotive.

LEFT: No.4472 working the 12.30 Bury-Rawtenstall service over the River Irwell at Burrs on Monday 22 February 1993 during its stay on the East Lancashire Railway. ***Tom Heavyside.***

ABOVE: All dressed up, but nowhere to go! The mood, perhaps, matching the inclement weather, No.4472 sits disconsolately at Llangollen station's platform, confined to static duties after the catastrophic discovery regarding the condition of its boiler. ***George Jones.***

RIGHT: Determined not to disappoint the many fans of *Flying Scotsman*, Llangollen Railway Society volunteers make the best of a bad job, ensuring that No.4472 looked as attractive as possible for the many visitors who still turned up to view the lifeless locomotive. ***George Jones.***

FKI Babcock Robey Ltd of Oldbury, West Midlands, having heard of the locomotive's plight, offered to assist with the overhaul of No.4472 and after an assessment of the stricken locomotive's condition, the company agreed to undertake the necessary work, *Flying Scotsman* being moved to the Company's Oldbury Works by road to facilitate the overhaul. Restoration of the boiler, involved a full retube, drain cock tubes shortened, along with minor attention to the firebox and a new smokebox, as well as the fabrication of a new set of boiler cladding. Babcock staff were assisted by Roland Kennington and other volunteers, all working relentlessly for over three months to ensure that the locomotive was ready in time to recommence its summer commitments.

One of the most difficult aspects of the repair, was to keep quiet the fact that the locomotive would be outshopped in BR condition, a promise that had been rumoured for some time. Nevertheless, on Thursday 22 July 1993, the metamorphosis complete, gleaming like a new pin, the born again No.60103 emerged from a 108-day overhaul. Resuming its tour of private railways and with a stunning and very controversial new identity, No.60103 was first of all off-loaded at Churston on the Paignton & Dartmouth Steam Railway on Sunday 25 July 1993. Transfer from the P&DSR to the Gloucester Warwickshire Railway at Toddington took place on 15 September, moving to the Birmingham Railway Museum at Tyseley on 3 November 1993, the Museum just having been given sole rights to use the locomotive on 'driver experience' courses each year until 1998, although existing agreements with other preserved railways would be honoured.

It was also during this period that a historic amalgamation took place - sealed by the two parties on 21 September 1993 - Sir William McAlpine's Flying Scotsman Enterprises and Pete Waterman's Waterman Railways merging - the plan being to strengthen and help both companies progress through the difficult times envisaged because of the British Government's plans to privatise BR. One aspect of the merger, was that Pete Waterman now owned 50% of *Flying Scotsman.*

ABOVE: In its stunning new guise and bathed in Autumn sunshine, No.60103 - complete with Kylchap double exhaust and chimney, German-style smoke deflectors and 34A shedplate - heads out of Toddington station on the Gloucester Warwickshire Railway on Saturday 9 October 1993. *Mervyn Turvey.*

RIGHT: Joint owner with Sir William McAlpine, Pete Waterman (left) with Roland Kennington on the footplate of *Flying Scotsman* during the A3's visit to the Swanage Railway in September 1994. *Andrew P M Wright.*

LEFT: On 17 April 1994, No.60103 backs onto its train at Llangollen, during a 'Friends of Thomas' event. One can only imagine what Sir Nigel Gresley - the locomotive's creator - would have to say about the unusual headboard being carried. ***Denis A Lewis.***

BELOW: On a normal service train, No.60103 waits to take its train away from Llangollen station, crowds gathering on Green Lane bridge in anticipation of a spirited start up the Dee Valley. ***George Jones.***

In the winter of 1993-94, following the completion of a programme of 'Footplate Experience' courses at the Birmingham Railway Museum, the second visit to the Llangollen Railway by the now BR Brunswick-Green liveried No.60103 took place, the locomotive arriving on 18 February. In the event, No.4472 stayed in north Wales longer than expected, a scheduled move to the Severn Valley Railway having to be aborted at the last moment due to a weight restriction being placed on a bridge over the Shropshire Union Canal by Clwyd County Council, preventing the locomotive's departure until 26 April. Forced to remain in Wales, No.60103 drew large crowds over the Easter holiday, more than adequate compensation for the Llangollen Railway, following the previous disappointment when the A3's boiler had been condemned.

From Llangollen, No.60103 moved to the Nene Valley Railway at Peterborough, the locomotive's arrival on 28 April 1994 having a remarkable effect on the seven-mile line, large numbers of visitors turning up at Wansford just to gaze at the locomotive even when not in steam. 'Footplate Experience' courses had been easily filled and additional days had to be inserted into No.60103's busy schedule to cope with demand.

LEFT: On 8 July 1994, No.60103 - disguised as sister A3s Nos.60039 *Sandwich*/60106 *Flying Fox* - headed the NVR's fine train of box vans. The reasons behind this transformation of *Flying Scotsman* to *Sandwich*/*Flying Fox* was to recreate the King's Cross-Niddrie Yard 'Scotch Goods' train using the superb rake of box vans preserved by the NVR. This event was but one of an increasing number of events featuring preserved locomotives disguised as long-scrapped classmates. *Chris Milner*/The Railway Magazine.

INSET: Earlier on 18 May 1994, as part of an 'old hands' day, former drivers, firemen and cleaners had been invited to the NVR to renew their acquantances with 'Scottie' and have a ride behind the locomotive. The group is pictured on the turntable at Wansford, with former owner Alan Pegler in the process of presenting a 'Driving Experience' certificate to 88-year-old Jack Storry of Kettering who had completed the course on No.60103 the previous week, almost certainly one of the oldest participants of such a course. *Mervyn Turvey.*

Typical of the complex arrangements that accompanied *Flying Scotsman's* many moves by road to different private railways in England and Wales between December 1992 and June 1995, is illustrated here. After a tortuous, three-day, 200-mile journey from the Nene Valley Railway, on 14 July No.60103 and tender arrived in deepest Dorset on the South Coast of England on two of Mike Lawrence's low-loaders for a visit to the Swanage Railway. On arrival at Swanage station, because the railway had recently lost its road/rail access point, *Flying Scotsman* was unloaded via a short section of newly laid track through the Goods Shed in the station yard.

ABOVE: No.60103 travelling along the M3 motorway in Hampshire on 14 July 1994 on the way to the Swanage Railway.
Mervyn Turvey.

INSET: A classic railway scene with the graceful lines of Sir Nigel Gresley's *Flying Scotsman* pictured at Swanage station in the summer of 1994, while in the background, Midland Railway 1F 0-6-0T No.41708, a veteran of 1880, impatiently waits to leave with the next service train of the day.
Andrew P M Wright.

All good things have to come to an end and after record-breaking attendances on the Swanage Railway, *Flying Scotsman* left the seaside on 18 September for a two-day journey north to the Severn Valley Railway.

This time, instead of being loaded through the Goods Shed, No.60103 was propelled by Class 25 diesel No.D7672 *Tamworth Castle* to the Swanage Railway's newly constructed railhead at Norden near Corfe Castle for loading onto lowloaders for the journey north, the A3 becoming the first locomotive to use this facility.

ABOVE: With the distinctive facade of the Railway Bell public house in the background, No.60103 waits at Kidderminster Town station on the Severn Valley Railway on 9 October 1994. *Norman E Preedy.*

INSET: One for the album! A father points out to his young son, the plaque commemorating *Flying Scotsman's* record breaking non-stop run during its exploits in Australia. *George Jones.*

After a sojourn on the Severn Valley Railway between 20 September-17 November 1994, No.60103 then moved to the Birmingham Railway Museum, departing on 11 January 1995. On 12 January, the locomotive commenced another turn of duty on the Llangollen Railway, the third visit in consecutive years. An exceptionally heavy schedule had been arranged, allowing the railway to promote a varied selection of events and ensuring a welcome influx of visitors.

With only a few months to go before No.60103's 10-year boiler certificate expired and despite rerivetting of the firebox foundation ring undertaken earlier in the month - as well as three 'caulked' repairs - the lap joints of the foundation ring continued to leak, causing concern at Llangollen that the locomotive might have to be withdrawn. However, trouble came from an unexpected direction!

On Saturday 22 April - the first day of a 'Friends of Thomas' weekend - at the end of a day's work, *Flying Scotsman* was derailed while taking empty stock into the loop at Llangollen Goods Junction. All 12 wheels of the locomotive were off the track, although the tender and stock remained on the rails. As the derailment was beyond the resources of the Llangollen Railway, an approach was made to Railtrack ECML for assistance. On Sunday 23 April, Bruff mobile lifting equipment was used to rerail the locomotive, the whole exercise being completed by the early afternoon, the locomotive then being taken back to Llangollen Yard for a mechanical examination and passed fit to resume duties.

The following day - 24 April - while the locomotive was under preparation for the day's work, steam was observed escaping from the side of the boiler, an investigation indicating that a crack had appeared at a point about head height on the fireman's side of the backhead. After a decision was made that an 'in service' repair was out of question, the locomotive was withdrawn and arrangements made for return to Southall. After travelling down to the West London Waste Terminal at Brentford on Mike Lawrence's road vehicles, on 9 June 1995 *Flying Scotsman* was hauled up the three mile long branch line to Southall Depot ready to commence a long awaited heavy overhaul.

LEFT: Photographed just after the derailment had taken place - sleepers still smoking from the fire being dropped - *Flying Scotsman* 'on the floor' with all 12 wheels in the ballast at Llangollen Goods Junction on Saturday 22 April 1995. *Mike Pearce.*

BELOW: Surrounded by steam, Ben Jackson - a Llangollen Railway volunteer - is pictured in the leaky cab of No.60103 a few days before the locomotive was finally withdrawn on 28 April 1995. *George Jones.*

CHRONOLOGY

On 11 April 1922, the first of H N (later Sir Nigel) Gresley's A1 Class Pacific locomotives entered service with the Great Northern Railway. With 180lbs/sq in. boiler pressure, 6ft 8in. driving wheels and three 20in. x 26in. cylinders producing a tractive effort of 29,835lb, they were designed to haul 600ton trains on the East Coast Main Line. The second locomotive followed three months later on 10 July. On the same day, a further 10 were ordered, the first of which was destined to become *Flying Scotsman*, the first locomotive to be completed for the newly formed London & North Eastern Railway.
Seventy-nine A1 and A3 Class locomotives were built between 1922 and 1935 (all except one of the original 52 A1s were later converted to A3s by fitting 220lb/sq in. boilers). *Flying Scotsman* is the only survivor and, apart from periods of overhaul, has remained in continuous service for 73 years running an estimated 2,500,000 miles. *This chronology is just the skeleton of a living legend.*

7 February 1923: Ex Doncaster Works. Works No.1564. Running number 1472. Cost £7,944. LNER Green livery. GN type 8-wheel tender No.5223. Boiler No.7693
22 February 1923: On display at Marylebone Station
24 February 1923: Allocated to Doncaster. Entered service.
25 June-4 July 1923: Comparative trials against ex-NER Raven Pacific No.2400, each locomotive operating three return journeys between Doncaster and London, resulting in the selection of the A1s as the LNER's main express passenger class.
27 December 1923-2 March 1924: General Repair, Doncaster. Running number changed to 4472. Named *Flying Scotsman*. Prepared for display at British Empire Exhibition, Wembley including LNER crest on cabside, brass trim to splashers and burnished tyres. (Ironically selected because of a fractured centre piston rod for which there was no immediate replacement!)
23 April-1 November 1924: First exhibition at Wembley.
23 March-19 April 1925: Heavy Repair, Doncaster. Coupled to K3 Class 6-wheel tender No.5378 due to limited exhibition space at Wembley.
9 May-31 October 1925: Second exhibition at Wembley.
16 November-28 November 1925: Light Repair, Doncaster. Coupled to GN type 8-wheel tender No.5223.
18 February-28 April 1927: General Repair, Doncaster. Variable blastpipe installed.
14 February-5 April 1928: General Repair, Doncaster. Variable blastpipe removed. Long travel valves fitted. Converted to LNER loading gauge. Coupled to corridor tender No.5323. Boiler No.7878 (new). Cabside numbers restored. Re-allocated to King's Cross.
1 May 1928: Hauled first non-stop run by 'Flying Scotsman' train King's Cross-Edinburgh (392.7 miles) in 8 hours 3 minutes with 386 tons tare. Drivers Pibworth and Blades. Tender axlebox overheated north of Newcastle which was cooled with slacker pipe; repaired overnight at Edinburgh to permit return run on 2 May.
April 1929: Co-starred in first sound feature film 'The Flying Scotsman' with Moore Marriott (driver) and Ray Milland (fireman).
23 April-8 June 1929: General Repair, Doncaster. Cylinders lined up to 19in. x 26in. Tractive effort 26,926lb. Coupled to corridor tender No.5324. Soot blower fitted.
17 January-15 March 1930: General Repair, Doncaster.
10 February-2 April 1931: General Repair, Doncaster.
6 April-20 May 1932: General Repair, Doncaster.
23 February-27 April 1933: General Repair, Doncaster. Boiler No.7804 (ex A1 No.2581).
19 April-30 May 1934: General Repair, Doncaster.
26 November-27 November 1934: Light Repair, Doncaster.
30 November 1934: High speed test run. King's Cross-Leeds (185.8 miles) in 151 minutes 56 seconds with 145 tons tare. Leeds-King's Cross in 157 minutes 17 seconds with 205 tons tare, including first authenticated 100mph for steam traction. Driver Sparshatt and Fireman Webster throughout. (At the time, the locomotive had completed 653,000 miles since entering service and 44,176 miles since last General Repair.)
27 March-18 May 1935: General Repair, Doncaster. Boiler No.7772 (ex A1 No.4471).
25 March-14 June 1936: Heavy Repair, Doncaster. Soot blower removed.
19 October-20 October 1936: Non-Classified Repair, Doncaster. Coupled to GN type 8-wheel tender No.5290.
25 June-24 July 1937: General Repair, Doncaster.
12 April-13 April 1938: Light Repair, Doncaster.
27 May-2 July 1938: General Repair, Doncaster. Coupled to streamlined tender No.5640.
6 March 1939: Re-allocated to Doncaster.
18 September-3 November 1939: General Repair, Doncaster. Boiler No.7785 (ex A1 No.2561).
20 November-23 November 1939: Light Repair, Doncaster. Automatic blow-down apparatus fitted.
10 May-11 June 1941: General Repair, Doncaster.
27 February-3 April 1943: General Repair, Doncaster. Black livery.
5 February-23 February 1944: Light Repair, Doncaster.
12 March 1944: Re-allocated to New England.
7 July 1944: Re-allocated to Gorton.
29 October 1944: Re-allocated to King's Cross.
11 November 1944: Re-allocated to New England.
5 December 1944: Re-allocated to Doncaster.
3 February-10 March 1945: General Repair, Doncaster.
25 April 1945: Reclassified as A10 Class.
20 January 1946: Running number changed to 502.
5 May 1946: Running number changed to 103.
18 May 1946: Light Repair, Doncaster.
18 November 1946-4 January 1947: General Repair, Doncaster. 94HP (220lb/sq in.) Boiler No.8078 (ex A3 No.2576). Tractive effort 32,910lb. Reclassified as A3 Class. LNER Green livery.
2 February-15 March 1948: General Repair, Doncaster. Maximum forward cut-off increased from 65% to 75%. 94A (banjo dome) Boiler No.9119 (ex A3 No.2505). Running number changed to E103.
17-30 December 1948: Light Repair, Doncaster. Running number changed to 60103.
4 November-16 December 1949: General Repair, Doncaster. Boiler No.9448 (ex A3 No.2747). BR Blue livery.
4 June 1950: Re-allocated to Leicester.
5 February-14 March 1952: General Repair, Doncaster. Boiler No.27015 (ex A3 No.60047). BR Green livery.
15 November 1953: Re-allocated to Grantham.
8 March-6 April 1954: General Repair, Doncaster. Boiler No.27074 (ex A3 No.60082). Converted to left hand drive.
13 April-22 April 1954: Non-Classified Repair, Doncaster.
20 June 1954: Re-allocated to King's Cross.
29 August 1954: Re-allocated to Grantham.
26 August-8 October 1955: General Repair, Doncaster. Boiler No.27007 (ex A3 No.60077).
7 April 1957: Re-allocated to King's Cross.
6 May-13 July 1957: General Repair, Doncaster. Boiler No.27011 (ex A3 No.60054).
10 December 1958-24 January 1959: General Repair, Doncaster. Boiler No.27044 (ex A3 No.60097). Kylchap double blast pipe and chimney installed (cost £153).
8 March-24 March 1960: Casual Light Repair, Doncaster.
6 July-9 August 1960: General Repair, Doncaster. Boiler No.27047 (ex A3 No.60100).
14 February-4 March 1961: Casual Light Repair, Doncaster.
21 November-16 December 1961: Casual Light Repair, Doncaster. Trough smoke deflectors fitted.
25 April-2 June 1962: General Repair, Doncaster. Boiler No.27058 (ex A3 No.60037).
14 January 1963: Withdrawn at approximately 2,076,000 miles after working the 13.15 King's Cross-Leeds service.
14 January-26 March 1963: Overhaul, Doncaster. Kylchap double blast pipe and chimney removed and single blast pipe and chimney fitted. Smoke deflectors removed. Outshopped in LNER Green livery with red backed nameplates and running number 4472 restored. Coupled to Corridor tender No.5325 (ex A4 No.60034).
16 April 1963: Sold to Alan Pegler for £3000. Entered service in private ownership. Based at Doncaster. Principally used for special trains on British Railways throughout Britain until October 1992.
20 April 1963: First public special in private ownership. Festiniog Railway Society Paddington-Ruabon via Snow Hill, where thousands turned out to see the engine.
November 1964-March 1965: Heavy Repair, Darlington. Boiler No.27020 (ex No.60041). Cylinder side casings painted green.
September-3 October 1966: Works visit, Doncaster. LNER crest on cabside restored. Second corridor tender (6000 gallon - water only - ex A4 No.60009. Cost £1000 plus £5000 for conversion and overhaul. Used on

most runs until No.4472's return from North America and occasionally until 1974.

1 May 1968: Despite signal checks and low water troughs, completed 40th Anniversary non-stop run King's Cross-Edinburgh in 7 hours 45 minutes (7 hours 17 minutes net) with 330 tons gross behind the first tender. Drivers Hill and Heron. Non-stop return run on 4 May 1968 with similar load in 7 hours 36 minutes.

November 1968-February 1969: Overhaul at Hunslet Works, Leeds. Boiler retube. Preparation for North American tour. American bell and whistle fitted, the latter was later replaced by a chime whistle in the USA.

August 1969: Light Overhaul, Doncaster.

31 August 1969: Last commercial excursion over British metals between King's Cross-Newcastle before commencement of American adventure.

19 September-28 September 1969: Approximate distance run since April 1963, 119,600 miles. Shipped from Liverpool to Boston. Cowcatcher and buckeye coupling fitted during crossing. Headlamp and steam generator fitted on arrival.

October-November 1969: First North American tour - Eastern and Southern USA. Stored at Slaton, Texas for Winter.

June-October 1970: Second North American tour - mid-USA and Canada. Stored at Toronto over Winter.

September 1971: Move from Toronto to San Francisco. Total distance run in North America approximately 15,400 miles.

August 1972-January 1973: Stored at Sharpe Army Base, Stockton, Sacramento.

January-February 1973: Purchased by Hon (later Sir William) Bill McAlpine. Shipped from Oakland to Liverpool via Panama Canal. North American accessories removed on arrival. Worked under own steam from Liverpool-Derby.

February-July 1973: Light Overhaul, Derby. Outshopped with black-backed nameplates, black cylinder side casings and cabside numbers restored. Moved under own steam to Torbay Steam Railway at Paignton.

22 September 1973: First commercial run on BR tracks since returning from USA between Newport and Shrewsbury.

October 1973: Moved to British Steel, Market Overton, joining GWR No.4079 *Pendennis Castle*.

1-10 August 1974: On display at Kensington Olympia as part of Burmah Castrol exhibition. Then moved to new base at Carnforth.

April 1975: New smokebox fitted at Carnforth.

August 1975: Appeared at Stockton & Darlington 150 Anniversary, Shildon.

28-30 November 1977: Co-starred with Dustin Hoffman and Vanessa Redgrave in Warner Bros film 'Agatha' as No.4474 *Victor Wild* and No.4480 *Enterprise*.

16 December 1977-6 June 1978: Overhaul at Vickers, Barrow. Estimated distance run since July 1973 59,000 miles. Diagram 107 (A4 type) boiler No.27971 (ex A4 No.60019). Long drain cock pipes fitted.

12 March-June 1980: Appeared at Liverpool & Manchester 150 Anniversary celebrations (Rocket 150).

1982-1984: Ran with A4 No.4498's corridor tender No.5324 in Green livery, but with Silver LNER letters while a new body was made for own tender chassis.

February/March 1983: Diamond Jubilee runs which included the East Coast Main Line from Peterborough to Edinburgh, electrification preventing the use of the line from King's Cross.

4 September 1983: Unofficially adopted by The Parachute Regiment.

20 November 1984: Hauled the Royal train carrying HM Queen Elizabeth The Queen Mother from Stratford to Woolwich. Cab roof painted white for the occasion.

March-27 December 1985: Seven-year overhaul at Carnforth. Estimated distance run since June 1978 135,000 miles. Boiler retube. Moved to Marylebone.

4 April 1987: Moved to Carnforth.

27 February-1988: Moved to Southall for overhaul in preparation for Australian tour. Estimated distance run since December 1985 13,500 miles. Driving wheels re-tyred. Air brake and electric lights fitted. Steam heat and AWS disconnected.

14 August 1988: Worked Marylebone-Stratford upon Avon-Marylebone Sunday luncheon train in painted, but unlined condition. Only public run in Britain since overhaul.

12 September-16 October 1988: Shipped from Tilbury to Sydney. Insured for £1,000,000.

25 October 1988: First public run in Australia.

October-December 1988: Victoria tour. Fitted with Australian chime whistle below the footplate until return to Britain.

December 1988-March 1989: New South Wales tour.

March 1989: Queensland tour to Brisbane.

April-July 1989: New South Wales and Victoria tour.

6 August-2 September 1989: South Australia and Northern Territory tour to Alice Springs. 4000 miles in 25 days.

8 August 1989: World record non-stop run by steam. Parkes to Broken Hill. 422 miles 7.59 chains in 9 hours 25 minutes with 535 tons gross. Seven British and Australian drivers used.

9 September-21 October 1989: Western Australia tour to Perth. Hauled 780 tons unassisted across the Nullarbor Plain. Total distance run in Australia approximately 28,000 miles.

12 November-14 December 1989: Shipped from Sydney to Tilbury via New Zealand and Cape Horn, completing the first known circumnavigation of the World by a locomotive.

December 1989-May 1990: Overhaul, Southall. Air brake and electric lights removed.

2 May 1990: First main line run following return from Australia, Paddington-Banbury and return.

25 October 1992: Last main line run (Ealing Broadway-Stratford upon Avon) before expiry of seven-year main line certificate on 27 November 1992. Estimated distance run since May 1990 12,500 miles. Steam heat reconnected. Commences tour of preserved railways.

26 October-1 December 1992: Birmingham Railway Museum.

3 December 1992-29 January 1993: Great Central Railway.

31 January-2 March 1993: East Lancs Railway.

4 March-30 March 1993: Llangollen Railway. Boiler inspection before first steaming revealed half of the flues leaking. Exhibited on static display.

April-July 1993: Overhaul by Babcock Robey Ltd. New smokebox, smoke deflectors, Kylchap double blast pipe and chimney fitted. Boiler retube. Drain cock pipes shortened. Outshopped in BR green livery. Running number changed to 60103.

25 July-14 September 1993: Recommences tour of private railways. Paignton & Dartmouth Railway.

21 September 1993: Flying Scotsman Enterprises and Waterman Railways merged to form Flying Scotsman Railways. Pete Waterman became joint owner of the locomotive with Sir William McAlpine.

15 September-2 November 1993: Gloucester & Warwickshire Railway.

October 1993: Birmingham Railway Museum given sole rights to use locomotive on 'driver experience' courses from October-December each year until 1998.

3 November 1993-17 February 1994: Birmingham Railway Museum.

18 February-26 April 1994: Llangollen Railway.

28 April-12 July 1994: Nene Valley Railway.

14 July-18 September 1994: Swanage Railway.

20 September-17 November 1994: Severn Valley Railway.

18 November 1994-11 January 1995: Birmingham Railway Museum.

12 January-6 June 1995: Llangollen Railway.

28 April 1995: Withdrawn due to cracked firebox. Approximate distance run on nine preserved railways since October 1992 30,500 miles.

6-9 June 1995: Moved by road from Llangollen to West London Waste Terminal at Brentford and then by rail to Southall Depot.

22 June 1995: Dismantling of the locomotive ready for major overhaul authorised.

23 February 1996: Purchased by Dr Tony Marchington for £1,250,000 in a handshake agreement with Sir William McAlpine. Major overhaul resumed.

3 May 1996: Boiler lifted off frames.

12 June 1996: Press Release from Flying Scotsman Railways announces the launch of the 'Flying Scotsman Association'.

24 June 1996: Alan Pegler accepts offer of Presidency of the 'Flying Scotsman Association'.

[This 'Chronology' was originally published in the March 1995 issue of *Steam Railway* magazine and has been subsequently updated.]

Compiler's Note: I am indebted to the many people who have assisted in compiling and correcting this record which has made use of material gleaned from a wide variety of authoritative sources. 'Estimated mileages' are educated guesswork, calculated with expert help - some could be conservative. Further research may provide more accurate figures.

I have only attempted to list what I feel are the most important or significant substantiated events, to include more would require a substantial volume, which, hopefully, will appear in the not too distant future.

I would be pleased to receive details of any errors or major omissions from the 'Chronology', via the publishers: Finial Publishing, 36 Park Road, Swanage, Dorset BH19 2AD, England.

EDWARD GARDENER

April 1997

At the end of a sombre day, darkness closes in as No.4472 *Flying Scotsman* crosses the Ribblehead Viaduct with the return 'The Lord Bishop' special on Saturday 30 September 1978.
D Trevor Rowe.

Through the resourcefulness of Alan Pegler in 1963, No.4472 *Flying Scotsman* was saved from the scrap yard. In 1973, the Hon 'Mr Bill' McAlpine successfully repatriated the locomotive from the USA after Alan Pegler had experienced financial difficulties. Surely, never again, could *Flying Scotsman's* future be in doubt?

Unfortunately, this proved to be the case and in the Summer of 1995, following the suspension of an essential heavy overhaul, national newspaper headlines proclaimed 'The train now rusting in a shed was once the most famous in Britain'.

As history records, the day was saved by Dr Tony Marchington who agreed to take on the mantle of responsibility for the locomotive in a handshake agreement with Sir William McAlpine on 23 February 1996. Thus, the future of the world's most famous steam locomotive was assured, *Flying Scotsman* being prepared for a new lease of life, stretching well into the third Millennium.